THE RICH MRS ROBINSON

THE RICH
MRS ROBINSON

BY

WINIFRED BEECHEY

Illustrated by Mary P. Taylor

OXFORD   NEW YORK

OXFORD UNIVERSITY PRESS

Oxford University Press, Walton Street, Oxford OX2 6DP

London New York Toronto
Delhi Bombay Calcutta Madras Karachi
Kuala Lumpur Singapore Hong Kong Tokyo
Nairobi Dar es Salaam Cape Town
Melbourne Auckland

and associated companies in
Beirut Berlin Ibadan Mexico City Nicosia

Oxford is a trade mark of Oxford University Press

British Library Cataloguing in Publication Data
Beechey, Winifred
The rich Mrs Robinson
1. Robinson (Family)
I. Title
929'.2'0942593   CS439.R/
ISBN 0-19-211783-1

Set by Promenade Graphics
Printed in Great Britain by
Butler & Tanner Ltd.
Frome, Somerset

Contents

A Time for Waiting

It is a very clever person who knows when he may feel himself to be rich.

'Soul, thou hast grown rich!' said the man in the Bible, 'pull down thy barns and build greater, take thine ease, eat and drink . . .' And God said, 'Thou fool! This night is thy soul required of thee.'

*   *   *

There never had been a time when I could not feel in my mother an idea that one day she would be rich. It was nothing to do with building greater barns or piling up wealth, but was a vision of a time of plenty, when she would be able to be extravagant and have a fling—give with an open hand, go to the theatre (taking a box, perhaps), have good clothes, real butter, roast chicken, and taxis everywhere.

My sister and I had no such vision, having succumbed early to our father's view of life and to his cry, 'We shall go broke! We shall all end in the workhouse!'

In 1919, when weary, disillusioned soldiers returned to face the Hungry Twenties and the great slump, our father was demobilized, and joined in the search for a home and a job. Day by day, leaving nothing to chance, he scoured the countryside for an empty house: a thin, eager man, with bright eyes, riding an old bicycle. Characteristically, he went his own way, his eyes not seeking 'To Let' boards, but curtainless, broken or shuttered windows, smokeless chimneys, and neglected gardens.

He had enlisted in 1914, but his battalion had not been

sent to the front. When he returned there had been a blurred photograph in the newspaper, '9th Hants Regiment disembarks after travelling 28,000 miles and serving continuously for five years in three continents'. But of where he had been and what he had been doing, we knew no more than what war itself meant. Among the treasures in his kitbag had been a ruby from the Ural Mountains tied in the corner of an old handkerchief; a piece of ivory from a mammoth's tusk; toe-rings; small glass bangles the colour of black treacle, encrusted with coloured beads and tiny mirrors; felt boots; Tsarist banknotes—thousands and thousands of roubles; and a song, printed in strange Russian characters on paper coarse and makeshift even to our wartime eyes.

Our mother, rather silent, and keeping her distance, had played the song over while my sister and I sat one on each of our father's bony, unfamiliar knees shyly fingering his puttees. When I asked him what the song was about, the bony, unfamiliar face had crinkled into a mischievous grin, and the deep-set eyes had sparkled.

'It's about a beautiful woman, and a man who loved her so much that he threw her into the river and drowned her. Now get off, and let your mother have a turn.'

This stranger, his thin face burned brown by the Indian sun, had invaded our world and filled it with restlessness and worry; our free, time-indifferent, unreal world, where there had been a mother and aunts, but no father and no uncles; a world of green and blue, cloud and wind, heat and biting cold, the Children of Israel, the Snow Queen, chilblains and toothache; with God looking down through a golden haze and the feathered wings of angels to protect us when there was thunder and lightning, or when the owls made blood-curdling noises, or when the wind rose frightfully in the night to make the giant elms—too near across the lane—creak and sway.

Now the landlord needed the cottage. In it we had lived for four of the five years our father had been away, and it was the only permanent home we could remember. Now, our father said, he must find us somewhere else to live, and he must find work, and we must all try to invent a game—that was the way to make money.

Invent a game! The need to invent a game, and the unaccustomed urgency of everything, weighed heavily upon me.

    *   *   *   *   *
       *   *   *   *
    *   *   *   *   *

2

THE cottage had been condemned before the war as being unfit for human habitation, and had sheltered Belgian refugees before housing us. It was a mile from the nearest village and three miles from the market-town, one of a pair built of mud and wattle and with brick floors, standing at the edge of a lane between cornfields. It had woodbine reaching up into the roof, and half an acre of garden with ancient fruit–trees and seas of stinging nettles. Water was drawn up in a bucket at the end of a long pole from a well by the front door, and there were two pigsties with an earth-closet attached.

The largest room had an iron stove with an oven, and a door opening on to a narrow curving stair which emerged into the two bedrooms above. Of the two other downstair rooms, one was so small that it had been used by the Belgian refugees as a larder; the other, whose open loft showed the sky through chinks in the tiled roof, had a stone sink and a copper and was called the wash-house.

There were no passageways, the rooms leading one from another.

Outside, the poverty and decay of the cottage was masked by the beauty of the giant elms, the fields, and high luxuriant hedges festooned with flowers or berries.

Inside, too, it was camouflaged. Our father had been addicted to sale-rooms, and the larger room was graced by his finds: the handsome mahogany table and the elegantly

'one of a pair'

curved chairs; the piano; and the green carpet with roses—all of which had been part of our parents' home since they were married. They had been married, our mother said, without a penny to bless themselves, and how she had grumbled when our father brought the chairs to their flat on a hand-cart, until he had scraped them clean and re-covered the seats. On the mantelpiece was a heavy, ornate clock, and on the crumbling walls hung pictures: Lady Townsend, with nutcracker jaws, and whiskers on her chin; Herodias, with a ring on her big toe, and brooding eyes; a court scene with monkeys dressed as lawyers.

The larder shelves had been taken down in the smaller room, and here our mother had put a deal table covered with a shaggy, green plush tablecloth, and hard wooden chairs. In one bedroom was her mahogany dressing-table and the brass-knobbed bedstead with its white counter-pane, and in the smaller bedroom our iron bedstead and a chest of drawers. She had made crisp white curtains with bobbled edges for the windows, and had somehow contrived to imbue the cottage with an impression of cheerful homeliness. It also breathed an air of originality and style as sure and as noticeable as that which came from our mother herself.

Our own poverty, also, was concealed. My sister and I had a certain cachet at school because we had 'come from London' and our clothes were left-overs from better days. When at first we went to church our mother wore—it seems incredible now—a long, duck-egg-blue satin dress right down to the ground, and a large hat swathed with duck-egg-blue satin to match; while my sister and I wore brown velvet dresses, the shantung collars and cuffs embroidered with scallops, French knots, and sprays of flowers.

The satin dress, which I thought silly, must have suited our mother more than my child's eye could appreciate. She alone in the family had very fine, black, wavy hair—real black, whose lights showed blue rather than the chestnut which is more usual. In the fashion of the day it was arranged in two soft wings, one on either side of a centre parting, then taken back and pinned carefully in two rolls high at the back of the head. She had a pale face and white skin. Her eyes, her best feature, were of the kind of hazel which is sometimes found with black hair and which often appears almost yellow in fading light: they were large eyes, gentle but full of little lights, their direct innocent glance rarely revealing the dry wit of which she was capable, and which she was not always suspected of possessing.

She would tell us a little legend—that she had once fastened her father's collar round her waist. Her father was a big man, and men's collars were cut rather low at the time; all the same, I think the fastening could have been for a moment only, during which she held herself in with all her might. When describing a person the figure is important, and the *expression* the figure wears is important (one can sometimes be quite adversely affected by the expression of a person's legs as they walk away). Whether it was the eye of love or just a lucky chance, our father caught exactly the expression of our mother's figure in a caricature he drew long ago, showing her standing beside him outside a fishmonger's shop. There was art in the representation of himself, too: in life, he was perhaps six inches taller than our mother, but in the sketch the man, as drawn, is barely as tall as the woman. Perhaps his essential humility caused him to cut himself down to what he considered to be the right size.

My sister and I would have been amazed to find that anyone could think of our mother as even good-looking, being to us, just our mother.

*   *   *

Most of the small scattering of cottagers nearby were farm labourers and lived rent-free: they kept a pig or two, chickens and rabbits, and grew enough vegetables and fruit for their needs. Our mother paid half a crown a week rent, and a pound a week to an old man to look after the garden and empty the bucket, but added to her eighteen and sixpence a week 'separation allowance' as it was called, by giving music lessons and doing dressmaking. Although there was scarcity of money, we did not equate this with poverty. When autumn came we had so many apples that we sold them for a penny a sack, and there were soon potatoes and other vegetables from the garden. With skimmed milk which we fetched from the farm only a penny a quart, there were always milk puddings; and then an occasional sheep's head, rabbit, or stew. And there was hard shop-dripping which we grated on to our bread with a knife at breakfast-time, and a wartime spread called honeysugar which came in a cardboard container; also remnant treasures from old strawberry-beds and rasp-berry-canes in our garden, and blackberries and mushrooms from the hedges and fields nearby.

The first winter at the cottage, I was ill with quinsy, and with breakfast on a tray my mother brought a boiled egg—and the next day, and the next day, and the next day. I accepted this treat with wordless pleasure. I knew I was being 'built up', and when the next day, looking quickly at the tray, I saw the egg was missing, I still said nothing; I guessed I had now been built up, and understood.

It was farming country, the richly fertile farming country of the Vale of Aylesbury, passing only slowly into the new century. The changing seasons were marked, as they moved hand in hand with the church's year, by a variety of small customs and the appropriate hymns: from Advent, when the earth's life lay imprisoned by frost, and

> O come, O come, Emmanuel,
> And ransom captive Israel . . .

was sung; to Easter, and the springing of the crops; through to Trinity, the earth's cycle having been completed by the hymns of Harvest . . .

> Grant, O Lord of Life, that we
> Holy grain, and pure, may be.

The walk to the village church seemed at first so long, and services so frequent, that it was as if, with the cottage for our shelter, we lived half out of doors and half in church, and the words we sang on Sunday,

> O ye Showers and Dews, Bless ye the Lord;
> O ye Lightnings and Clouds, Bless ye the Lord;

O ye Ice and Snow, Bless ye the Lord,
Praise Him and magnify Him for ever . . .

we soon knew and understood very well. We became well
acquainted with the wind that 'bloweth where it listeth',
and 'Who shall abide His frosts?' found a ready response in
my heart. Oh, the biting, biting cold of those winters at the
cottage! Sometimes, on a raw dark morning when we had
come home late the day before, the pail under the sink
would be empty. Then we might see our mother struggling
in a womanish way with the well's heavy lid, which had
become frozen down. Anxiously we would watch her out
there in the misty half-light, inexpertly chipping with a
hammer and chisel at the ice, till at last the lid was freed,
and she fixed the pail to the pole, lowered it into the well,
and drew it up swaying and slopping with water for the
kettle and the morning cup of tea.

But there was all the time in the world in the long, silent,
lamplit winter evenings: sitting by our mother at the hard
table with its green cloth while she machined, playing with
the contents of her work-basket—'tidying it for her'; or
folding spills and cutting lavatory papers with fringed or
scalloped edges from old church monthlies; or watching
her turn back the tablecloth, and enveloped in a meaty
steam, her eyes pleased and interested, make a little
ceremony of dealing with a sheep's head she had been
simmering on the oil-stove—the brains put aside for
frying, the tongue peeled and pressed into a little brown
dish with some of the juice, and the meat scraped off the
bones and put with some more of the juice into a glass jar
for brawn.

When the weather was really cold we had a fire alight in
the other room and washed and undressed before it. On
one side our bodies scorched in a heat so fierce as hardly to
be borne, while on the other side the draught coming from

the stairs, through the immense keyhole, and from gaps round the ill-fitting latch door, cut with icy purity. Unable to settle comfortably, we moved this way and that, scorching our cold side and cooling our scorched side.

All the rituals of bedtime were carried out here: the rubbing of chests and backs with camphorated oil, the brushing of hair, the telling of stories, the saying of prayers, and (yes) the singing of the evening hymn, in three parts.

The prayers and the evening hymn were no formality to my sister and me, but a very real and necessary preparation for the hours of darkness. It would not have occurred to us to ask to be protected from burglars; it was the elm trees across the lane, and fire. Often we would get out of bed after our mother had left us and say a few supplementary prayers. If it were cold, if the floor was hard, so much the better—God would know we were trying. There were so many many ways in which the cottage might catch fire in the night, and every one had to be mentioned: a chance spark from the embers in the grate, our mother's bedtime candle with its guttering, wavering flame—or she might not turn the lamp out properly—she was so reckless. Then the cat, Knottytrotty, a half-Persian stray,

'secretly smouldering?'

with her freakish long hair: she sometimes slept in the ashpit beneath the dying fire and there had been occasions when a piece of red-hot ash had fallen on to her back. Might she not secretly be smouldering, and rub against some paper in the night?

When we were ready for bed our mother lighted our candle with a paper spill from the jar on the mantelpiece, and gave us each a brick which had been heating in the oven and was now wrapped in an old vest. Then we were prepared to face the stairs and the first plunge between the sheets. There is something specially cold about cold sheets which are also slightly damp, and in spite of the hot bricks, which by now would be throwing out a comforting smell of scorched vest, it needed a strong effort of will to push the first foot down the bed.

Sometimes when our mother came up she would take me, the ever-wakeful, into her bed to warm it for her, while by the light of a candle she read, and cracked bull's-eyes. Faithfully I hugged her arm, watching with stiff, pricking eyes her eyes moving so eagerly from side to side, side to side, down the pages of *The Storyteller*, which the aunts brought from London when they came. The candle flickered wildly in the draught, tormenting the shadows and the knots and whorls in the old wooden planks overhead. And the pool of melted wax round the candle's wick overflowed like tears and trickled slowly down the candle, congealing as it went. With a child's ever-constant realization of death, I thought how one day our mother must die. Would they perhaps just let me keep one arm, I wondered?

In the night my sister and I would sometimes hear our mother cry out in her sleep as if in terror, but we soon became used to it, and took it as a matter of course.

✳   ✳   ✳

As far as my sister was concerned, I must have seemed twice a cuckoo in the nest: once when I was born, and again when I returned after spending a year at the beginning of the war in London; I had stayed with an aunt on my father's side of the family, perhaps as a playmate for her little boy, my mother and sister living meanwhile with my father's parents.

Now, although only two years older than I was, my sister treated me in a very grown-up way. Her intelligent, widely-spaced brown eyes were stern, and she pursed her lips. The only game she would play with me was one she had invented herself, called Ghostly Rides, which took place when we undressed upstairs. At the shedding of each

'vaguely unclean'

garment I carried her on my back to and fro, and round and round the bedrooms.

She was in any case a very grown-up child, never rushing about playing 'He', or 'Sheep, sheep, come home!' during playtime at school, but walking quietly with her friend Flo, talking. Enclosed in grown-up mystery they walked side by side, and often my sister would receive notes from Flo ending, 'PS. Don't tell anybody.'

At my sister's request, I slept at the edge of the bed we shared, as being vaguely unclean. Secretly I knew this to be justified; I had a past, of which, as far as I knew, no one but I was aware.

From the moment I had left my home to stay with our aunt I had become wicked.

My cousin had already started to attend school when I arrived on the scene, and soon I accompanied him. He was proud of me, my hair done in a pigtail for the first time. We called for his friend Sidney, and then all three stepped out along the pavement to school, the two boys whistling, and I between them pursing my lips hoping passers-by might think I was whistling too.

Once having passed through the school gates they left me, and I set about doing everything my aunt had told me not to do.

First, I went to the water-fountain, and capturing the metal cup which was tethered by a chain, I managed to reach up and squirt myself some water, which although I was not in the least thirsty, I drank. I then sought the lavatories, which my aunt had warned me never to use, and although I did not need to, I did use them. Finally, I saw on the ground, all in the dust, what appeared to be a toffee which had fallen from someone's mouth (or had it perhaps been spat out?) It looked moist and sticky, as if melting, and already had quite a coating of dust. It must be very infectious, I thought, picking it up and putting it into my mouth. It tasted so nasty that I nearly spat it out myself, but I could almost taste the infections, so sucked on to the last gritty sliver.

My aunt was very particular as to which children we should or should not play with. There was a little girl called Becky who for some reason did not qualify for our friendship, and when the novelty of my presence had begun to wear off, and my cousin reverted to Sidney's company only, as far as school was concerned, deliberately disobeying, I stopped on my way to school to call for Becky. Then one day I climbed on to a chair and lifted down the rosewood tea-caddy from the dresser where it was kept. It had two compartments, one for my cousin's money and one for mine. I took out all my money. There was ninepence-halfpenny. After all, I told myself, it was not stealing, it was my own. But the deceit of it made me feel as wicked as a murderer—magnificently wicked.

That day at school I showed Becky my money and told her I was going to spend it all. She did not ask where it had come from but promised to take me to the shops when we came out of school in the afternoon, and help me.

It must have been winter time, because it was dark when we reached the shops; and the noise, and the brilliance of the lights against the black sky, made the place seem an exhilarating hotbed of evil. Recklessly we went from shop to shop. It seemed as if we could buy anything in the world with my ninepence-halfpenny. Becky's eyes were bright with daring as we bought sweets, lemonade, more sweets, and a little celluloid doll which Becky fancied. Then it was over, and we went home, and the emptiness of my side of the tea-caddy was never mentioned.

One day my mother came, and told me that she had found a little house where we could all be together, and that I was going back with her; but turning to my aunt I buried my face in her skirt, and said I didn't want to go—not knowing why I said such a silly thing, but noticing how surprised and pleased was my aunt, and how hurt my mother.

There my wickedness ended. Back again in the orbit of my primitive allegiance I was myself again, and that other little girl disappeared.

3

OUR mother was the eldest of five sisters. Their mother had died young, and although their father had married again, the aunts still looked to our mother for stability, and often visited us. All high-spirited, each a queen-bee in her own right, they would mill round the cottage having hurt feelings, singing, quarrelling, crying, and teasing us.

Their grandmother on the father's side had been Irish and of good family—her mother being of the family of Ormonde. At eighteen she had run away from home to marry a Welshman, Edmund Davies. He was twenty-four years her senior and at that time a travelling carpenter and cabinet-maker; yet an old daguerreotype shows nothing of the seducer in the kind, thoughtful, Pembroke face: 'a gentleman', one would have said. Perhaps Mahala, his young wife, had been the wild one. Disowned by her parents, she died when only twenty-four years old, having contracted puerperal fever after the birth of our grandfather, her fourth child. When her family heard of her death they had asked to take the children. But, our mother would relate of her grandfather, 'he was too proud'. He brought them up well, and gave them each a good education.

Because our mother had been 'the best needlewoman in seven schools', she was apprenticed to Worths, the Bond Street and Paris dress designers. She still kept the sample-books into which had been tacked the work which had won her her title: pages of specimens of every kind of buttonhole beautifully executed; gussets, plackets, gathers set into bands; print patches perfectly matched, flannel patches, calico patches; different methods of darning, and hedge-tear mending . . . When she married, her wedding dress was made at the Paris workroom, 'a costume in fine white serge with a gored skirt just touching the ground; it was really very smart. All round the bottom of the jacket and on the collar and the revers was embroidery: purple, mauve, white, and silver-thread, because I was in half-mourning for my mother. I wore a big white felt hat with a white ostrich feather round it, and Daddy wore a fancy yellow waistcoat. We were very much admired!'

Our eldest aunt, Aunt Winifred, had qualified for the Civil Service on leaving school, but had failed to pass the medical examination. She had a weak heart, and was reputed to have had rheumatic fever three times. But things seemed to have happened three times over in that family with such suspicious frequency, that automatically, to be on the safe side, I credited her in my own mind with twice only. She did not look weak, being something like our mother in figure, but plumper, and her face was always pink. Her head was noticeably large, with a high broad forehead; and like many people with large heads, she had very small feet (her mother had 'taken a two'). She had brown hair, direct blue eyes, a wide, well-shaped mouth, and beautiful teeth. She shared with our mother the gift of a lovely smile, which she sometimes employed later in business—'. . . he gave me a lovely smile, and I gave him a lovely smile back: I sometimes smile like that myself, and know just how much or how little it may mean.'

At that time also I remember her saying there had never been a man with whom she had seriously disagreed in business who had not made her cry, lent her his handkerchief, and in the end lost his case.

She worked in the counting house of a large London store, where later she was to become the company secretary—'a man's job'. Now, feeling herself to be the practical and hard-headed one of the family, she would go debt-collecting when she came to stay, determined that our mother should not be put upon 'because she was weak'.

'One-and-six for making a blouse like that—all those little tucks and button-holes—and then not paying you! And that Mrs Thomas, does she think you can risk your neck in the dark on that dreadful bicycle just to give her children music lessons for nothing? No, I shan't be *rude*, you know I never could be, *but I will be firm!*' And pinning on her hat, she would set out along dusty lanes and across muddy fields in her high-heeled shoes, very determined and very firm.

She was the present-giver, remembering our birthdays with the fairy stories of Hans Andersen and the Brothers Grimm, the Arabian Nights, and Little Lord Fauntleroy, which, with our mother's old Sunday school and Band of Hope prizes, and the horrific adventures of the Children of Israel, wove themselves into my life, mingling with the screaming of the cottagers' pigs at slaughter, crimson sunsets, the feverish confusion of sore throats and colds, enormous moons, the Germans, smouldering haystacks, and the relentless cold stare of stars in winter, to make my world a place of grandeur—mysterious, fiercely exciting, frightening, and beautiful.

Aunt Kate was the next aunt, and a very different kind of person, a person of secrets and mysteries; for one thing (my sister told me), when our mother wrote to her she addressed the letter to 'Mrs Hansley-Boyle' which, as we knew, was not really her name. My sister questioned her.

'Where do you live?'

'You mustn't ask me that.'

'But where *do* you live?'

'Well, shall we say I live in a little tent on Hampstead Heath.'

She was the only aunt who would let me try on her hats and come into her bed in the morning; there she would tell

me stories about Daisy Flea and Oscar Bug, and help me
with my collect for Sunday school; it was so much easier
the way she said it—

'O *Lord* we be*seech* Thee *mer*cif'lly to *hear* us, and *grant* that
we-e-e-e . . .'

But she herself always seemed to be in trouble; it would
be her hat, exaggeratedly large for the sake of fashion,
which blew off when Mr Turnham's hired cart brought her

'it would be her hat'

the three miles from the station—even then it had to sail
away over the hedge—and the songs she sang were of a
melancholy strain:

> Nobody knows when I am lonely;
> Nobody cares if my heart breaks . . .

and

> Nobody cared if she laughed or cried,
> Nobody cared if she lived or died;
> In the great city that has no pity,
> In the great city that has no heart . . .

While, in the long hot summer days, our mother was
catching up with her dressmaking, this aunt would lie in

the long grass in a far corner of the garden and we would fan her with rhubarb leaves while she told us stories about our mother when she was young.

'. . . she used to have a lovely hat with poppies on it, and she used to wear such lovely blouses, so dainty. When she was going out we felt very proud of our sister Amy, and we all crowded round her to have a good look. She used to say, "Don't touch me! Don't touch me!"

'But your father never stopped worrying her. They met on the train, and she is so weak—just like a jelly wobbling in its mould when someone keeps on at her.' (The weakness of our mother, Jelly, and the firmness of herself, Rocky, was a favourite theme of Aunt Kate's. Sometimes when my sister and I were prevailing upon our mother, Aunt Kate would join in with, 'Be firm, Jelly! Be firm!', or sing a mocking little song,

> First she said she wouldn't,
> Then she said she couldn't,
> Then she said, 'Oh well, I'll try'.)

'. . . and the things those two got up to! There was the time your father invented a drink called Non-Tox. They got quite clever at making it and bottling it. It was doing very well, but your father has no head for business and in the end he sold the idea for almost nothing at all.

'Then another time he left his good job in the City to set up a workroom to make umbrellas with strap handles instead of the crook handles they always were then; he had your mother there managing the girls, and she caught fleas and brought them home to you young babies—it was dreadful! An old lady used to look after you in the daytime, and when your mother came home, you (nodding towards me) were so pleased to see her that you screamed for the rest of the night. So they gave it up; they couldn't have that happening.

'They lived almost entirely on herrings at that time, I believe. I remember your father even made up a song about herrings, something like,

> Aren't things cheap, Bill,
> Up the Harrow Road,
> Herrings six for tuppence, Bill,
> Shan't we get a load . . .

'Then it was bicycles, and of course he was right in a way, they were the coming thing, but he went into partnership with someone near Southampton who ran away with the money. So he took a job as a milkman, with rabbits as a sideline of his own—your mother used to skin them; I forget how many she could do in an hour—the way she worked!

'But your father is a really good man, whatever else he might be, and *really* good men are few and far between . . .

'He was always joking: we called him Jokey, he did make us laugh. And he had lovely hair; your mother always said she married him for his hair.'

Then she told us thrilling tales of how our great-great-great-aunt Beck had had webbed feet, and how our great-aunt Sarah had been so small when she was born that they had put her into a pint jug, and how our mother had been a seven-months' baby and had been christened in the bedroom, and had had pneumonia three times.

'She couldn't walk till she was three, and because of having had such a bad start she got round-shouldered, so she had to sit on an orange-box at the meal-table till she was sixteen. Our father used to come along behind her and tap her on the back and say, "Hump!"—it did make her wild. But they were very strict about straight backs in those days. I remember when I called for my school-friend in the mornings her mother used to say to me, "Remind her to keep her back straight, won't you, dear." When my friend grew up, her back was so straight that she looked as if she might fall over backwards.'

'Mummy must be very delicate,' I suggested nervously.

'Delicate? *No*. Very very strong.'

No one could have desired a more attentive and appreciative audience than my sister and I. Assiduously we fanned, my sister sending me every now and then to pick a fresh supply of rhubarb leaves.

We were gratified to learn that we ourselves were not without claim to distinction.

'For the first six months of your life,' my aunt said dramatically, turning towards my sister, '*hair grew on only one side of your head!* In the end your mother took you to a hairdresser but he told her not to worry, that it would come right in the end, and so it did.'

'What about me?'

'Well, you were a poor little thing, only five pounds seven ounces, with the cord wound three times round your neck, and black in the face. You had to be brought to life. And then, for the first six months, you cried day and night without stopping. Your poor mother! And she was pea-green with anaemia and had raging toothache the whole time. Your father had got tonsillitis, but he's like that. You *should* be very lucky, because as you were coming into the world an old man called Mr Coppick in the flat above was leaving it. He had no one of his own, so your father sat with him while he died. When I came to see your mother the next day, there was your father sitting by her bed making a wreath for old Mr Coppick out of Canterbury bells—goodness knows where he'd got them from. Of course an ordinary bunch of flowers was not good enough for your father, he had to make a wreath. The floor was covered with wire and Canterbury bells. He'd forgotten all about you!

'For a long time you were very small, but pretty, just like

a little doll at one-and-eleven-three with your curls and your blue eyes. And then, one day . . . *you suddenly began to grow!* And after that—well, just look at you.'

It was so lovely and warm in those endless afternoons, so comfortable and drowsy. Sometimes Aunt Kate's voice would stop, and we could see she had fallen asleep. Then we would wander off to sit and read or ponder in some private place. There were several places, apart from the pigsties, to which we could retire: one was a grassy disused cess-pit, Abraham's Bosom, just big enough and deep enough to contain one child unobserved if sitting down. Several of the old apple trees had good sitting places, too; in particular those whose branches stretched right over the hedge. There one could gaze up almost into the heart of the elms, or see, over the further hedge, acres of wheat: a molten blue-green ocean heaving sluggishly to every breeze, yet each ear thrusting upwards upwards separately, full of its own individual life. Nearby, a row of lilies grew by the mouldering end wall of the cottage. Standing there hot and still in the sun, so waxy, so astonishingly beautiful in their white and gold, they filled the air with a sweet, languorous scent—the smell of high summer. Accustomed to thinking of the piece of wasteland opposite my aunt's house in London with its butterflies and long soft grasses as a kind of fairyland, I was still overwhelmed by the bounty to which we had come, and by the knowledge that I could pick anything, do anything, that it was all free.

'Webbed feet! How funny she must have looked,' I said to my sister in bed one night, with a vison of an old woman walking down the lane with a poke-bonnet and dressed in black, with ducks' feet flapping in and out at the bottom of her skirt. 'And fancy them putting a little baby into a cold jug. Whatever did they do that for?'

'You don't have to believe everything she says, it's just

the way she talks,' said my sister. 'Probably it was so small that they thought it would have gone into a pint jug. Do you remember that time when she was ill here and Grandma Davies had to come? Well, she had been going to have a baby herself. But you mustn't tell anybody. You must never tell *anybody*. They think I don't know. Its father was killed at sea. That's why she never goes to Grandpa's.'

Even though she was part of our lives and we loved her, Aunt Kate shocked my sister and me to the core. To tease and embarrass me she would sometimes mutter a terrible grace as she sat next to me at the meal-table:

> The Lord be praised, my belly's raised
> A foot above the table;
> And I'll be *damned*, if I'm not crammed
> As full as I am able.

It was awful.

'The Lord be praised' (taking the Lord's name in vain), 'my belly's raised' (our mother would never never have used, nor allowed to be used in her presence, such words as belly and breast; for belly she would have said stomach, and for breast, bust or chest. Later my sister and I would whisperingly refer to our breasts as our developments—but only in private). 'Damned' was a word never used in our home and rarely at that time heard by us outside it, except when it occurred in readings from the Bible.

It was just too awful.

But another grace with which Aunt Kate teased me was a temptation:

> We thank Thee, Lord, for this our food,
> Although 'tis very small;
> If there'd been more, we could have eaten more,
> But thank the Lord for all.

For some reason the last two lines were very satisfying to me. I longed to say them. I could not quite manage to deceive myself into pretending, however, that I did not understand perfectly well that they were making fun in what was a prayer, and therefore taking the Lord's name in vain. But could I not perhaps just say the last two lines over to myself now and then, just think them? It was a temptation, but I knew even this would be 'taking the Name of the Lord thy God in vain', so with many a backward glance and with great regret, I renounced them.

Aunt Kate had certain resemblances to our mother: she was much the same size, with the same sloping shoulders and the same eager pitter-patter footsteps. Her eyes, however, were brown. Her hair was sometimes brown and sometimes a deep auburn, and I accepted and shared her apparent astonishment at its puzzling behaviour. But it was in the expression of her eyes, even more than in her colouring, that she differed from our mother.

I do not know what kind of work she did then. I have an idea that she worked in a library, although she was one of those people who find spelling difficult; and she was strongly left-handed, which was considered a great disadvantage in those days. I have a memory so strange that I can hardly believe it. It is of me sitting at some kitchen table cleaning out a jam pot with a long spoon, with aunts quarrelling and weeping around and above me: then out of a silence a voice, which said (of Aunt Kate), 'She ran up the street in her night-dress, carrying the till.' I have puzzled over that remark for most of my life but it never occurred to me, while I could, to ask its meaning.

Aunt Kate liked to try on our mother's clothes, and would say, 'Amy's mantle has fallen upon me! I *am Amy*. Don't you think I look like Amy? Don't you think I am *like* Amy?'

And with the unthinking cruelty of childhood we would reply, 'No, not as good.'

'Ah! But remember this: your mother was born good; it is easy for her. *I was not born good!* It is not as easy for me. There is one thing, I will never marry a poor man. I will never work as Amy has had to work.'

In a family brought up in Spartan traditions and with a high regard for the therapeutic qualities of will-power, Aunt Kate was very sympathetic, and would come and sit by us if we were not well, saying little, just keeping us company. But we were not often ill, our ailments usually yielding to our mother's standard remedies—tincture of rhubarb, bread poultices, and camphorated oil—together with will-power, and that other mysterious source of strength which helped us to bear our misfortunes almost with pride:

'A sick headache! You take after me, a *Davies*.'

'A sore throat! *Just* like your father.'

It had been Aunt Kate who, when doing the bedrooms, had been discovered gaily emptying the slops out of the windows: 'But in the country, Amy. Surely in the *country* . . .'

The third aunt, Aunt Dorothy, was different again: she wore pince-nez and was considered plain by her sisters, her brown hair, though fine, being straight, and her nose *retroussé*. She was, however, very ladylike; taller than the others, and proud of her figure and hands.

'Remember, breeding tells,' she would say to my sister and me, in that voice which always held, underlying it, the tone of a querulous child. 'Always remember that. *Breeding tells!*' And she would try to smooth the accents we were fast acquiring with a verse she had composed for the purpose:

> *Down* the lane, we *found* a *cow*, and *how*
> Are we to drive it *out*.

How strange it seems to me
To find a *cow* so near the sea.

She, more than any of the aunts, was liable to break what our mother called 'the congenuity', although she could be very entertaining, and would sometimes sing and play her way right through our store of music at one sitting.

Bitterly resentful of her father's second wife, Aunt Dorothy had been so consistently rude to her that when it came time for leaving school and starting work in a bank she had been found lodgings, her stepmother, with some reason, having refused to bear with her any longer.

'No wonder he has trouble with his new wife,' Aunt Dorothy now assailed our mother. 'It's his punishment for breaking his promise.'

'His promise?'

'Yes, he promised our mother that he would never marry again, that day she came home from seeing the specialist. You weren't there. She told him that the specialist had said she had only six months to live. She said to him, "You won't have anyone else, will you. Promise me you'll never marry again, that there'll never be anyone else." And he promised.'

'No,' said our mother, 'it wasn't like that, you weren't there, you were only a little girl. You couldn't have been more than eight years old. She had come back from seeing the specialist and was lying on the sofa, and she told Dadda that she had only six months to live, and he went out into the kitchen and was crying into the roller towel. And she said to me, "Go and say something to him", and I said, "I can't". That was all that happened. He did it for our sakes.'

Marjorie, aloof, the youngest and later to be perhaps the best-looking of all the sisters, blue-eyed and brown-haired, was the only aunt still living at home. She was less than eight years older than my sister, and as we were neither babies nor contemporaries, was inclined to treat us with disdain.

As for our father, his forebears had been born and bred, generation upon generation, in and about the parish to which we had come. His great-great-uncle had been a corn and hay merchant and market gardener, using also part of his premises as a village shop, and another part as a bakery. Childless, and a widower, he made a bargain in his old age that if our grandfather would look after him until he died, he would give him—except for a few legacies—all he had. The bargain was faithfully kept, the old man living on well into his eighties.

Our grandfather had started his working life in the comparative peace of a solicitor's office, and it may have been that he was not suited to the multiplicity of new skills and duties which later fell upon him. As his responsibilities increased, and the stern role of Victorian father was laid upon him, he became silent and taciturn. His eight children called him Whishty-whisht ('Whishty-whisht! Here comes old Jo!') and it is sad that the only kind words I ever heard spoken of him in the family were spoken by our mother, who always referred to him, as 'that much mis-understood man'; but then, she always did stick up for men.

In effect, he provided free bread to a number of poor families in the surrounding hamlets, who could never afford to pay and were never expected to. Flour sacks bearing his name carpeted a number of kitchens; and his ladders, seasonal tools, and intrepid little ratting terrier, were borrowed as if by right.

He was a religious man, his religion being flavoured with austerity; in his old age he would tricycle three miles to worship at a neighbouring church rather than attend the one fifty yards from his home which he considered was becoming 'too high'.

The discipline to which he subjected his own children was very severe. Seated in the choir-stalls one Sunday morning with his four brothers (his father and uncle being in the row behind), our father discovered he could make a circle on his handkerchief by pressing his collection penny into it. Whereupon he spent the rest of the sermon-time decorating the bottom of his surplice with a pleasing and complicated design . . . to find his father's eye upon him. When he reached home his father needed only to point to the staircase for him to know that he must go dinnerless to bed.

Our grandmother, gentle, poetry-writing Mercy, who also came of farming, gardening, church-going stock, would perhaps provide a good example of submissive, heavy-laden, Victorian wifehood. She had come from Bedfordshire, of a family almost Quaker-like in outlook. One sister had joined the Salvation Army, and years later I found an article recording her death at the age of forty-two, in which she was referred to as 'the Mother of Cardiff', having been largely responsible for the foundation of a home for unmarried mothers.

Mercy had started work as a companion to someone my father always called Granny Wheeler. The two women must have been great friends, because the highlight of the year for Mercy's children was to go, two at a time, to stay with the old lady.

So it came about that sometimes in the early morning two bright young faces would peer round Granny Wheeler's bedroom door.

'Can we come into your bed, Gran?'

'Why, yes my dears.'

'Can we do your hair, Gran?'

Then she would put aside her Bible, and they would brush, comb, and put up her hair, and sprinkle her thoroughly with scent from the bottle on the dressing-table.

'And what would you like for dinner today, my dears?'

'Spare ribs of beef, please, Gran.' My father had no idea what this was, but it sounded important, and they would go to the butchers and buy spare ribs of beef, and bring it home for Tilly, the little maid, to cook.

'Now, what would you like to do this morning, my dears?'

'Have a bike out, please, Gran.' So the kind old lady would hire bicycles, and later sit patiently on a milestone by some quiet road, watching the little boys as they dashed to and fro for the rest of the morning.

Every Friday evening, Tilly set out with a basket under her cloak with provisions for the poor, but sadly, at the end of Granny Wheeler's life, so much of her substance had been given away that she had difficulty in providing for herself.

4

IT was very quiet in our lane, almost deserted. There was nothing to suggest in that dusty white strip stretching serene and empty to the horizon that it had once been the ancient route of fighting men, trodden by thousands of marching feet.

A hundred yards or so from the cottage the lane was intersected by a similar white strip, and quite early in the mornings a band of children would straggle past on their way to school. They came from, and round about, a village beyond us called Bishopstone, and most of them had already walked a mile or more before reaching our lane. They were spoken of at school as 'the Bishopstones'.

In spite of the witness of gravestones in the churchyard that we were of their kind, the Bishopstones treated us as foreigners, and would not let us walk to school with them. They would drift up the lane, run past us, then stop and look back. If we tried to advance, they would turn on us fiercely: 'Sling yer bloomin' 'ooks!'

The way to school became familiar ground and full of secrets and treasures; marked here by a spindle tree, its berries so strange among the hips and haws, and there by a root of white violets and some dry teasel heads over a

'It was very quiet in our lane'

field-gate and behind the hedge. A large white house, with lodge and coachman's quarters, stood back from the road in well-kept grounds. This was the home of Lady Smyth, the aunt of Baden-Powell. She seemed to dress always in black, and irreverent Aunt Kate had named her 'The Lady of the Flowing Robes'.

My sister, already established in the village school, was in the middle room. I was put in the Infants, and my teacher was called Mrs Cooke.

Mrs Cooke was formidable, stout, and thickset. She wore a long black serge skirt, a black blouse with the high-boned neck made fashionable by Queen Alexandra, steel-rimmed spectacles, and elastic-sided boots. Her hair, sparse and iron-grey, was drawn up into a tight little knot on the top of her head, and she had a false fringe which sometimes, to her pupils' embarrassment or delight, slipped revealing a patch of naked, white scalp. Did people's hair go from the top and come out of their faces when they grew old, I pondered.

Mrs Cooke had taught many of the children's parents, and it was her pride that no child ever left her class unable to spell the word 'chrysanthemum', having learned in this way not to be afraid of long words but to break them up into syllables.

'I met one of our Tommies home on leave from the front line the other day,' she told us (and I remember still the pride in her voice). 'Do you know what he said to me? He said, "I haven't forgotten how to spell chrysanthemum, Ma'am. C-h-r-y chry, s-a-n san, t-h-e the, m-u-m mum, *chrysanthemum!*" '

I had 'gone up' in my last school, and was already able to write out all the multiplication tables. Now, as an Infant, I started from the beginning, but everything was so new and so different that I did not think of this as a retrograde step.

Mrs Cooke used her own face as apparatus for teaching her pupils to count. '*One*', she would point to her right eye, which her pupils would explore with interest; '*two*' she would point to her left eye; three, was her nose; four, her mouth, and five, her chin. When the children were working out their sums they would look up from time to time and gaze thoughtfully at Mrs Cooke's face. Then lips would move, and heads wag from side to side, up and down, as their calculations were made.

Our teacher had taught my father how to knit, and I think it likely that he learned with the very same wooden needles, also that he used the very same off-white string-like yarn which was knitted up and unravelled over and over again by successions of grubby little fingers. Sometimes the stitches of an earnest scholar would become so tight on the needles as to be immovable, and being unable any longer to keep up with Mrs Cooke's relentless, 'In-round-out-off! In-round-out-off!' he would burst into tears.

Although not thinking of it in such terms, I could see that the school I had attended previously was provided with altogether better equipment. Instead of the slates with wooden rims, and the slate-pencils which squeaked so tortuously,we had written on rimless boards with chalk. Marks made with slate-pencil are not quite as easy to erase as those made with chalk. At my new school I watched with interest a classmate mustering all the dribble in his mouth and spitting it on to his slate, and I remember the look of virtuous satisfaction with which he regarded it, before scrubbing away with his slate-rag as industriously as any little housewife.

Occasionally the headmaster would visit the class and roar up and down the gangway between the rows of desks. Without in any way comprehending what it was all about, we took on what we felt to be the pose most likely to please: sitting up straight (yet not so straight as to seem cheeky); arms folded behind our backs as we had been taught; alert, although not self-consciously alert (yet not so expressionless as to appear gormless or daft). The headmaster exploded this way and that like a thunderstorm, and we were terrified—but not too terrified, because, after all, that was the way of headmasters, and ours was a good and kindly man.

Most of the children here, precocious in such matters as country children often are, seemed to have sweethearts, even in the Infants. I was courted by the son of a market gardener, who expressed his feelings with gifts of black- and red-currants on the bough, and the choicest of ripe gooseberries nearly as big as pennies, the like of which I think I shall never taste again. We would sit together in a

grassy corner of the playground, feasting luxuriously. In
that little home of ours we must have eaten pounds and

pounds and pounds of fruit;
he was always a good pro-
vider. He wore buttonholes,
which seemed sometimes
almost as big as he was: a
spray of lilac, or even labur-
num; a cabbage-rose of
deepest crimson, whose
large, close-petalled head

'a good provider'

would become too heavy in the heat of the classroom and
droop, flooding the stale air with the warm, rich, winy
sweetness of its decay.

✳   ✳   ✳

Soon after we came to the school it was decreed that
schoolchildren should pick blackberries to be made into
jam for the soldiers. The headmaster had scales on his desk,
and a mountain of pennies spread out to pay a penny a
pound. Bashful and ashamed, my sister and I, inexperi-
enced in the art of blackberry-picking, went up to the desk
with our offering for the soldiers—a grubby paper bag
containing the harvest of a day's anxious search—'almost a
pound' of small, squashed blackberries, their hearts' blood
seeping quietly away through the bottom of the bag. Then
the Bishopstones went up, carrying between them several
baskets and bags lined with cabbage leaves. 'Over eighteen
pounds!' But that was not all. Everyone could see the
quality of their blackberries; how large, juicy, plump and
shining they were; blackberries which grew in places only
the Bishopstones knew of. With eighteenpence, cautious
smiles on their faces, they returned to their seats.

Some of the Bishopstones were ragged and untidy, and
some of the girls were reputed to have no knickers. Some

32

had holes in their boots, and at playtime would stand in the puddles pacifying their chilblains. But they were the only ones who knew the secret places where fraucups grew, and in spring came to school with tired bundles of the flowers hanging over their arms, for the teacher. They brought sandwiches for dinner, and some had dreadful colds, spreading out their wet, eucalyptus-smelling handkerchiefs on the pipes in the dinner hour to dry.

My sister and I went home for dinner, even though it meant running most of the way. My sister ran always a little ahead gasping at intervals, 'We shall be late! I know

'*a distance beyond our home*'

we shall be late!' while I plodded along behind her as best I could, grumpy and rebellious.

On Fridays a fish-cart came to the village and left a piece of cod in the meat-safe hanging outside the back door of Mrs Cooke's house. It was for her friend, Miss Paradise, who lived a distance beyond our home in the direction of Bishopstone. My sister and I delivered it, and although probably neither Mrs Cooke nor Miss Paradise realized, delivering the piece of cod was the bane of our lives. At the end of morning lessons we sang grace:

The eyes of all wait upon Thee, O Lord,
And Thou givest them their meat in due season . . .

and marched decorously into the cloakroom. Then the
rush began. Grabbing our coats, we were over the road and
ready waiting on Mrs Cooke's doorstep by the time she
arrived, and when she had handed over the abhorred
clammy package we were away like two greyhounds off
the leash.

Those pieces of cod had dreadful experiences on their
way to Miss Paradise's house: lost in the snow, squabbled

'the abhorred
clammy package'

and wrangled over, dropped in the
dust, and pursued by flies. By the
time we arrived panting and wild-
eyed at our destination, the fish
was almost naked, its wrappings
having been lost, bit by bit, on the
journey.

It never occurred to us to tell
Mrs Cooke that it was all we could
do to get home, have dinner, and
be back at school in time, without
running errands—or to ask for
permission to be late. Nor did our
mother, sympathetic to our dis-
tress, seem to have thought of it.

We Infants had our singing lessons in the cloakroom or
'the porch' as it was called, Mrs Cooke finding the note
with a tuning-fork. Anyone willing to sing alone was
hoisted on to the wash-basin in the corner. Looking down
one day upon my classmates' upturned faces as I stood,
legs stretched almost to bursting point to straddle the
slippery basin, a feeling came over me that it was a very
strange thing to do.

The same feeling came over me later when I had 'gone

up'; at the end of the day, when even the sun's rays slanting in through the diamond-paned windows were dusty, and fagged and grubby we knelt on the hard narrow seats of our twin desks, facing the back of the class, 'hands together eyes closed' to sing

> Peace, perfect peace,
> In this dark world of sin . . .

5

IN the cottage joined to ours lived a Belgian refugee, 'Madame', and her baby, 'Rappypoupins'. Madame earned money by doing bead-work which our mother tried hard to help her to sell. She could often be seen sitting at the door of her cottage on a chair whose seat, once of cane, was now just one big ragged hole, playing with her baby or threading beads on to wire which she bent into flowers or formed into cake-baskets.

Now Madame's husband made his appearance in the lane—a Belgian soldier in uniform—small and dark-haired with a mild expression and a peaked pill-box hat. He dug part of our garden, as he said to repay our mother's kindness to his wife. It was a different kind of digging from that practised by our old gardener, and raised the level of the ground several inches. He then presented us with a photograph of himself in uniform with his wife and Rappypoupins, and took them away.

Their place was taken by a farm labourer and his wife, and their children, Elsie and George. The father, John Rogers, was a slow, quiet countryman whom I do not remember ever having heard speak. The mother was quiet too, brown-eyed and gentle and given, as Elsie would relate, to going off into a dead faint. She gave help to two of the neighbouring farmers' wives when required.

Their cottage was smaller than ours, having, apart from the tiny scullery, only one room downstairs. Here the uneven but well-scrubbed brick floor was protected for much of the day by sacks, while by the fireplace was a rag mat. Mrs Rogers borrowed one of our mother's saucepans when her sister came to stay because, Elsie said, her aunt was used to having her vegetables cooked separately. In spite of this lack of worldly goods, however, we did not think of the Rogers' as 'poor people' any more than we thought of ourselves as 'poor'. No one who had seen Elsie setting out for Sunday school, bright as a button in her little round black felt hat which sometimes had a pink ribbon and sometimes a pale blue one gathered round it, her boots glittering with polish, could think of her as poor.

In no time Mrs Rogers was teaching our mother how to ride a bicycle, the bicycle itself being bought second-hand from Elsie's aunt, who worked at the munitions factory in the town and the light from whose bicycle lamp wavered across the curtains at half-past six on dark mornings.

To my sister and me nothing could have been stranger than to see our mother trying to ride a bicycle. We crouched at the edge of the lane and watched, as she came wobbling along—to fall off over and over again with agonizing inefficiency. Although almost everyone's mother cycled into the town, the idea of our mother doing the same seemed against all the laws of nature, and her journeys to nearby villages to give music lessons, often in the evening and lighted only by her paraffin lamp, became the subject of many an anguished prayer.

Later her bicycle was to develop sinister clicking noises, a circumstance which seemed to our manless household as desperate and hopeless as when her sewing-machine had tension difficulties.

We had playmates now. The Rogers' kept a pig, but our sties were still empty and my sister and I had one each for a house. Sometimes a gypsy-dark head would appear poised precariously over the top of the wall separating the two cottages at the back, as Elsie's toes clung to her footholds.

'Play in y'Pig?'

I shook my head. I decorated my Pig with beech leaves; it was private.

'Play in the spinney?'

We played in the spinney near the cottage for hours, climbing the trees, pruning them of dead twigs, or making

houses; or we swung on field-gates, and balanced along the top of them; or collected cow-parsley in a sack for the Rogers's rabbits; acorns, and snails (or oddy-doddies as Elsie called them) for the pig, and blackberries and mushrooms for our mothers and sticks for their fires. George, one boy among three girls, ran backwards and forwards in the lane trailing the trundle his father had made

'Play in y'Pig?'

from a tin lid threaded through the middle with string, or pinged our heads with a pig's bladder.

Any small occurrence was a cause for excitement; the threshing-machine's visit to the field opposite was quite an event. We children would stand by for hours looking to see the families of pink baby mice brought to light as the men lifted the sheaves from the old stack.

One day the farmer came by bringing home a 'war horse' whose nerves had been affected by the noise of the guns. We saw them coming along the lane, the horse rearing, and jerking its head angrily from side to side. We stood perfectly quiet, our backs against the wooden palings of the cottage. The farmer was riding with the utmost gentleness and skill, and as he came nearer we heard his voice, hypnotic and soothing:

> 'C—p c—p c—p Come along then old gal,
> C—p c—p c—p Come along then old gal,
> C—p c—p c—p Come along then old gal,
> C—p c—p c—p Come along then old gal . . .'

They were making better progress now. Horse and rider moved as if on springs, light as thistledown. We were motionless, scarcely daring to breathe, and the patient, soothing voice continued without a break,

> 'C—p c—p c—p Come along then old gal,
> C—p c—p c—p Come along then old gal . . .'

But perhaps the sustained stare of four pairs of eyes was too much. The spell broke, and with a violent movement the horse reared, threw its rider, and bolted.

6

IN uncertain circumstances, and with a future impossible to predict, we passed our days reassuringly enough within a framework of the seasons, which followed one another with unfailing regularity and brought at predictable times pancakes, holly and mistletoe, Lenten abstinence, willow-catkins, and familiar collects, hymns, and prayers; and another framework suggested by words and expressions our mother revered, such as methodical, will-power, ladylike, and firm.

She was already giving us piano lessons, and now taught us songs which we sang together when we went out to tea with her. Some of the songs I thought so silly that I could hardly bring myself to sing the words, but it would not have occurred to me to say so, or to have refused, and I would stand glumly at my sister's side, one hand in hers as required of me, singing

> A hat of green, and gloves of grass
> Would make me like the trees;
> They'd think I was a little leaf
> Just blown there by the breeze . . .

and worse:

> Yellow daff-o-dilly in your golden gown,
> You have wakened early from your bed of brown.
> Did you hear the birdies, (*birdies!*) while you were asleep?
> In the garden calling, Pee-eep, pee-eep, peep.
>
> Yellow daff-o-dilly, you are very sweet . . .

'Yellow daff-o-dilly, you are very sweet'

However, I thought the words of one of my primitive piano pieces, fortunately not performed in public, so sad that I could not even practise it without weeping:

> Underneath the gaslight's glitter,
> Stands a little fragile girl;

39

Heedless of the night winds bitter,
As they round about her whirl.
How her little heart is sighing,
In the dark and weary hours;
Only listen to her pleading,
'Won't you buy my pretty flowers?'

'Underneath the gaslight's glitter, Stands a little fragile girl'

Our mother did dressmaking for Lady Smyth, and when there was a fitting my sister and I were invited to tea. While Lady Smyth submitted to the pins, we played in the garden, and after tea, with grave courtesy, our hostess usually asked my sister if she would recite for her. With the same grave courtesy she listened to my sister's ardent rendering of the poem they were learning at school just then—a poem which, although none of us seemed to notice, was not altogether a happy choice, and which in any case always made my blood run cold with horror:

Stitch . . . stitch . . . stitch,
In poverty, hunger, and dirt;
And still in a voice of dolorous pitch,
She sang the song of the shirt.

My sister and I were soon invited to join the Young Helpers' League, part of the village's effort to support the work for destitute children of the philanthropist Dr

Barnardo. The meetings were held in the small reading-room near the church, and there we made garments which would later be sold in aid of Dr Barnardo's Homes.

Mrs Cooke, assisted by Miss Paradise, usually presided. She sat on the table beneath the swinging oil-lamp, her feet in their elastic-sided boots planted firmly on the trunk in which garments were stored, and helped us with our work. At school she ruled with an iron hand, but here she tended to fraternize, making heavy jokes. But the children were not to be drawn; it was like being invited to fondle a lion at the Zoo.

A poor needlewoman, and the youngest member of the Young Helpers' League (only accepted to keep my sister company), my garment was a pillowcase. The room was quiet, the firelight flickered, and as we sewed one of the girls read us a story. Nevertheless, in spite of a pleasant feeling of virtue, I found forcing my needle through the stiff calico heavy work, and my garment soon became speckled with little spots of blood.

Miss Paradise, a pale shadow of Mrs Cooke, did small tasks for her, and conversed with her in confidential tones. 'The wood on the fire popping like that, dear. Doesn't it remind you of our boys in the front line?'

At the end of the evening Mrs Cooke took the pins from her mouth and stowed garments and sewing gear into the trunk. Again seated on the table beneath the lamp, she opened a large prayer-book, adjusted her spectacles, and read:

Lighten our darkness, we beseech Thee, O Lord, and by Thy great mercy defend us from all perils and dangers of this night . . .

and thus protected we felt no fear of the dark walk home.

*　　　*　　　*

When summer came we attended the annual garden party in Lady Smyth's grounds in aid of Dr Barnardo's Homes. Custom had made the children of the village feel as at home, and as rightfully there in Lady Smyth's garden, among the cedar trees and roses, as they did in church, among the stone carvings and stained-glass windows, although in both places they knew how to behave. It was really quite a treat just to walk on the smooth, soft, springy lawns in the sunshine and under the cedar trees; it was so spacious there and so restful.

In one part of the garden was a strong, well-made swing, and there a girl was entertaining a group of young men, handsome in the bright blue of wounded soldiers. Gently she pushed them to and fro on the swing, bending over them and laughing. So romantic was the scene, and the young men so splendid in my eyes, like creatures from another world (and wounded!), that quite a glow was kindled within me.

There were stalls of all kinds, selling cacti in little pots from Lady Smyth's greenhouses, a penny each; bundles of spills, pin-cushions, and lavender-bags; and on the main stall the garments—night-shirts, aprons, petticoats, chemises—all made by the Young Helpers during the winter evenings.

A well-known speaker was to make an address, and after refreshments had been served from trestle tables we assembled at the foot of wide steps which led to the stone terrace and portico. A group of people sat in chairs on the terrace, the visiting speaker prominent, her hat generously decorated with sprays of artificial flowers. Before giving her talk she was handed a box of sweets which, standing on the steps, she scattered gracefully handful by handful to be scrambled for by the children.

My sister and I got none. We were so slow, and the other children—already practised at garden parties—pounced

with such swiftness and skill, that by the time we realized
what was happening all the sweets had disappeared as if
they had never been. However, when the speaker began
her address we listened with our usual earnestness. She was
talking about poor people in London: 'I went into the
room . . . and all I saw . . . was a dirty, greasy table . . . and
on it . . . an old crust of bread.'

Obediently imagination illustrated for me her words. I
saw an uninhabited room. It had three sides and no
windows and oddly enough was on the stage of the village
hall. It was unfurnished but for the dirty, greasy table with
its old crust of bread. I saw the table very clearly. It was the
deal table at home but without its green cloth, and dirty
and greasy . . . But why was it dirty and greasy? Because
the people were very poor, and very hungry. They would
be weak with hunger . . . too weak to clean the table.

My mind's eye experimented with a picture of our
mother in such a case. Before my horrified gaze she
crawled slowly in from off-stage and advanced upon the
dirty, greasy table on all fours, a soapy cloth in her hand.
Weakly she tried to pull herself up one of the table's legs,
only to fall back. Again she tried . . . But the vision was too
awful. Sick at heart I dismissed it and turned my attention
to the old crust of bread, which rested upon the table,
slightly to the right of centre.

It was the familiar curved crust, tending to be burnt
black outside, and difficult for loose front teeth; the kind
of crust our mother always said was enough to feed ten
strong men. But this crust had been left on the table; no
one had eaten it up . . . But then hadn't I heard of people
being *sick* with hunger? Oh why did people go to London
if they were poor!

Once while living with my aunt in London I had
adventured with my cousin too far and we found ourselves
in 'poorer parts'. A woman standing in a doorway had

shouted at us—even my cousin had been frightened—and partly this, partly something about those squalid streets with their listlessly blowing paper and broken windows— the suggestion of degradation and despair—had left a horror and fear which haunted me. Why had the people stopped trying? Had they never tried, or was there something about being poor which made them stop trying? *Should we get like that if we became poor?*

Oh why did poor people go to London to those terrible streets! Much, much better to stay in the country—even set out to walk there if they were in London already . . .

(My mother and my sister and I could make a house of dead grass and leaves in a deep, dry ditch. I knew of a suitable one nearly opposite the spinney. We could live on things like beech nuts and blackberries till we got too weak and then we could creep into our house in the ditch and cover ourselves with the dead grass.

'Are you all right, duckie?' our mother would say to my sister.

'Yes, thank you, Mummy,' my sister would reply bravely.

'And you?'

'Yes, thank you, Mummy.'

'Not hungry?'

'Not so very hungry, thank you, Mummy,' my sister would reply.

'And you, duckie?'

'Not so very, *very* hungry, thank you, Mummy,' I would say, not to be outdone.

And then we should die. There would be no poorer parts for us.)

7

LADY SMYTH taught in Sunday school and drove herself to church in a governess cart drawn by a fat little pony called Betty. We ourselves spent much of the day on Sundays walking to and from church. We came to know almost everyone there and almost everyone knew us and all about

'walking to and from church'

us, and there would be discreet smiles and nods for our mother as we came in—she perhaps in her duck-egg-blue satin, and we in our brown velvets with the hems let down.

The first rows of pews had hassocks, and doors with brass doorknobs. I would have loved us to be in a pew with a doorknob, but it was no good, our mother always led us to one half-way up the church with no door and a wooden kneeler. Although when we arrived at the cottage I had spent the sermon time at church crawling about under the pews, sometimes getting lost and surfacing in the wrong row, I soon began to give attention to the service, singing the hymns we knew, wrestling with the psalms, and trying to understand the lessons and sermon.

I cannot remember a time when I did not understand perfectly well the principle behind the helpful expression, 'figuratively speaking' so often used by our mother and the aunts, considering with kindly tolerance Isaiah's angels with six wings, and mountains in the psalms that skipped like rams. But 'the ten commanderments' I took very seriously indeed. A cloud of guilt hung over me for the rest of the day when one Sunday morning waiting for the school door to be unlocked I succumbed to the temptation of sliding on a little frozen puddle ('Remember that thou keep holy the Sabbath Day'), and I was often worried by our mother's deviations. For instance, playing 'The Destiny Waltz' on a Sunday. Or singing (on any day) 'Let the blessèd sunshine in . . . ' 'Blessèd' was a word used in the Bible, about God, so might not its use in an ordinary song about sunshine be 'taking the name of the Lord thy God in vain'?

'We shall all sin,' said the Vicar, gazing down from the pulpit, 'inevitably, because of the frailty of human nature.' He developed the theme at some length. The only thing to do, I decided, would be for us all to die right away, before we had had time to make bad worse, and I would have accepted euthanasia for the whole family then and there had it been offered.

It seemed to me sometimes, as we knelt on the hard wooden kneeler with our prayer-books open before us, that people did not really take praying seriously; that there was a curious gap as if somehow here also 'figuratively speaking' were involved. They asked for things, 'Thy kingdom come . . .', 'Defend us, O Lord . . .', 'Grant us Thy peace . . .', 'Lead us, Heavenly Father, lead us . . .'. But Aladdin had been so much more practical in his requests to the Genie of the Lamp.

On a day of catastrophes I knelt in the garden behind the hedge and prayed: 'Please God find our kitten. Please God don't let our mother's bike k-k-k any more.' Almost at once I heard the kitten mewing, as coyly it pushed its way through the long dead grass; and then I heard my sister's joyful voice on the other side of the hedge as she rose on the pedals of the bicycle: 'The bike's not k-k-k-ing any more!'

The immediacy of God's response quite startled me. It was not long, however, before I began to realize the possibilities of my discovery.

For instance, getting up in the morning. If there was one thing worse than getting into bed at night, it was getting out of it again in the morning; leaving the snug hollow I had made, warm with the warmth which only the proximity of another living body can give, *really warm* for the only time in the twenty-four hours, to dress in teeth-chattering, fumble-fingered cold and darkness. Once, inspired by some fairy-tale, I had come down very early to try to light the fire; pushing damp sticks between the bars not even realizing that the ashes must first be raked out, and precious matches had been wasted. Now, as a start to my new life, I saw a better way.

I said nothing to my sister, but the next day went to and from school and finally to bed carrying my secret with me; when she slept, I knelt by the small grey square which was the window. 'Please God, when we get up in the morning, let there be a nice fire burning downstairs.' Freezing cold, but full of hope, I climbed back into bed and lay down beside my sister.

I awoke early and remembered. Carefully getting out of

bed, I picked up my clothes and felt my way downstairs. Could it really be that I should be greeted by warm, crackling flames? Could it really be that God . . . ?

I reached the bottom of the stairs and quietly unlatched the staircase door.

'Could it really be that God . . . ?'

Except for the small grey patch which was the curtained window, there was complete darkness—no light, no warmth, no fire. In contrast to my hopes, the dark, deserted room seemed even colder than usual—alien, hostile, still belonging to the night. Regretfully, but with no real surprise, I accepted that evidently God did not work like that after all, and crept back upstairs to bed. It was disappointing, but somehow I had not really thought it could be like that. I was even a little relieved; perhaps, after all, things were better as they were.

8

It never occurred to me during those waiting years that the life we were leading, ordered and seemingly secure, might leave something to be desired as far as our mother was concerned, nor that it held for her anything of hardship. Just once, very late at night, I thought I heard her crying in the room below, but by the morning I could not believe that so strange a thing had happened; I had dreamed it, it was the owls. But I remember how we went to every concert held in the village, every social, and every lantern lecture, regardless of the weary walk home and the cold welcome of our cottage; and I remember particularly well the day we went to the pictures in the town when 'The Scarlet Pimpernel' was being shown at the Town Hall, because then the walk home seemed so very, very long.

It was well after ten o'clock before we stumbled out of the Town Hall, bleary-eyed and dreamy but still anaesthetized by the last romantic close-up. That warm pink glow in our hearts lasted almost till the lights of the town were left behind, and we knew that until we saw the Bugle Inn in the distance, there would be only three houses on the right and four on the left until we reached our lane. The only light now came from the sky, but we were no

'The only light now came from the sky'

more worried by the darkness than were the small nocturnal animals which rustled in hedge and ditch as we passed.

After the first mile my sister and I began to droop, each clinging to one of our mother's arms. We had passed the first house on the right . . . soon we came to the little bridge over the brook which we had crossed all those hours ago . . . then a place where we stopped in wonder, in spite of our tiredness, to watch hundreds of little frogs hopping across the road on some mysterious errand of their own . . . then on the right a lodge surmounted by a golden star, the Star Lodge, shadowy and silent, and the interminable high stone wall within whose shelter Louis Bourbon once lived in peace and in safety from his countrymen . . . then a shape to the left . . . another . . . another . . . another, set further back, and on the right a second lodge, while we followed a long, long path where moonlight filtered eerily through a thick row of trees, throwing stripes for us to walk over . . .

All this time our mother was keeping us awake with stories of when she was a little girl.

'. . . and then, coming home from school sometimes, I would climb up a bank where there was a lot of water, and say to them, "I've been a good sister to you, and now I'm going to drown myself."

'They were dreadfully upset. They would all stand there crying, and saying, "No! No, Amy! Don't! *Please* don't!" . . . and then they would start promising me all their things; their dolls, and bracelets, the pictures in their bedrooms . . . in the end I would come down and tell them, "Perhaps not today." '

'Tell us about when you said the baby had struck a match.'

'Well, one day our mother went out for a few moments and left me alone with the baby, who was sitting in the high chair. I couldn't have been very old myself, because the baby must have been Winnie, but I can still remember thinking, *Now what can I do while she's gone!*

'And do you know what I did? I might have set the house on fire! I got a box of matches, and I struck a match. And then I didn't know what to do with it, so I just held it up to the clock on the mantelpiece and it made a brown mark on the glass and went out. When our mother came back she saw the mark at once but I told her the baby had done it.'

Our mother paused, and we stumbled on in silence.

'. . . But my mother believed me because she couldn't

think I would tell her a lie, although it always puzzled her, I know, how the baby could have managed to do such a thing.

'She used to give us the stick, and one day I pretended to faint, just to see what she would do. She was dreadfully upset . . . I just *had* to open one eye to see what she looked like. Oh dear, she was cross then!

'And then I remember one day I said to her, "Other mothers kiss their little girls when they go to school, and their little girls kiss them back. Today we are going to kiss you, and you must kiss us." '

'What did she say?'

'She put her cheek out ready, and said, "Come on then, and be quick about it." '

'I think your mother was horrible,' said my sister suddenly, 'horrible and cruel.'

'Not really, parents were different in those days, and she had to be firm. It's a big responsibility bringing up five little girls, especially five like us, and Dadda would just have spoilt us all.'

'What did *he* used to do?'

'Well, he used to love us all standing round him while he played the piano and sang funny songs . . . and hymns . . . he used to like that one, "The Dying Thief Rejoiced to See". They don't seem to have it much now-a-days,' and she sang,

'The dying thief rejoiced to see
That fountain in his day;
And there would I, as vile as he,
Wash all my sins away.'

'Every Friday he used to bring our mother home a book. Dickens was their favourite, and they used to read it and laugh together over the funny bits. At Christmas they used to go into the other room and read, and our mother would peel walnuts for him, while we played with our Christmas things in the kitchen. We each had an orange, an apple, six nuts, a new penny, and our Christmas toy.

'When it got near to Christmas time, we would open our money-boxes and get out our money, and our mother would take us to buy our Christmas toy. Once she took us to the West End, to see the toy-shops there.

'All the way to the shops I was so happy. I knew what I was going to get, a great big doll.

'The dolls often had real hair in those days, and beautiful clothes. My doll, I knew, would be wonderful. It would have a wax face, and long hair, and oh dear, I don't quite know what I did expect. But in the end, what I had in my box was not enough. All I got was one of the little wooden Dutch dolls they had then, with black paint for hair.

'I remember standing there looking at it, hardly believing, thinking to myself, *Is that all it's going to be!*'

'Didn't your father and mother want you with them in the other room?'

'He did. Once I heard him say, "Let them come, Emily, I love to hear them laughing." But she said it was so seldom they could be together. She was very fond of him.'

'Your mother was horrible.'

'No, she had a lot to worry her. You understand these things as you get older. She was always afraid that Dadda would lose his job, because when they were paid at the end of the month all the men in the office went and had a drink together, and he got drunk—some men are like that.

'When it got time for him to come home, he didn't come, and our mother had to get Winnie and me out of bed, and we had to dress and go to the station and watch the trains as they came in. There he would be, fast asleep, and we had to make him get out, and get him home. He was always sorry afterwards, but it never made any difference.' (Was this our dignified, stern-faced Grandpa?)

'Although my mother always tried hard to hide it from me—she was a very proud woman—I always knew how it hurt her that he should degrade himself. And I believe she thought that someone whose mother had been a titled lady should have known better how to behave: she was very innocent in some ways.

'Because of her worry that he might lose his job she was always very economical, trying to save money for a rainy day. She grew spinach in the garden—great pans full, and it all cooks down to nothing. We had bread and lard instead of bread and butter, and sometimes I would have to go to the fishmonger's for just *one herring* for Dadda's tea. O dear, how I hated having to say it! "A penny herring, with a soft roe, please."

'Later on my mother got so afraid that Dadda would lose his job that she took me away from school earlier than she would have done; she thought that at any rate I might be earning, if anything happened. When she told him what she had done he was so ashamed and upset that he wept. I think that was when he stopped.'

The voices of my sister and our mother came sometimes sudden and loud, with a jolt, and sometimes as if from far away. Sometimes I would let my eyes close, then I would remember the Bugle, and open my eyes again, and again strain ahead. The Bugle . . . we should see it in the distance . . . there would be a big white square . . . the Bugle . . . Surely *that* was it. Surely what I saw *was* whiteness, not just a lighter part of the darkness? . . . Was it? . . . Was it?

And then, at last, there the Bugle was, standing fairly and squarely before us, and the road turned the corner and branched off into our lane. After that I must have been walking in my sleep, because I never remember getting home.

No concerts or lantern lectures, not even the fairy-stories of Hans Andersen and the Brothers Grimm, were as entertaining and interesting to my sister and me as when our mother was a little girl. Even when the little match-girl froze to death I did not weep into my pillow, as I did when I thought of how our mother had saved all the currants out of her suet pudding for a treat at the end, and then her mother had made her give them to Aunt Winifred because it was bad manners.

But how could *our mother* have been so awful saying that the baby had struck a match and not owning up when her mother believed her. Yet somehow it was very pleasant thinking about how wicked she had been when she was a little girl, and the strange thing was that she was not a whit diminished in my eyes.

It had been the same when my front tooth had been loose and I had grizzled and grizzled for days, until in the end our mother had intervened. 'Let me look at it, I won't touch.' But when my mouth was trustfully opened, she had grasped the tooth, twisted it firmly, and pulled it out. I might have been expected to distrust her for life, but 'God is not mocked', neither are little children, and although momentarily outraged—she is awful—a sound instinct kept my faith in her absolute and complete.

And the matter of the redcurrants.

Sometimes after church on a summer evening we walked a long way round on our way home, taking a path which ran by market gardens where there were rows and rows of soft fruits. Our father's uncle was a market gardener; it was some of the best market gardening soil in the country, and the redcurrants especially were wonderful . . . and some of them might well have been Uncle Bill's, but which?

'*These* must be Uncle Bill's, he wouldn't mind,' our mother would say comfortably, pausing to eat some of the best fruit as it hung splendidly, translucently red, in the evening sun. And later on . . . '*These* must be Uncle

Bill's . . . *These* must be Uncle Bill's . . .' (But how, we thought disapprovingly, could she be sure?)

And then how she bought a *Rainbow* comic to keep her Sunday-school boys quiet—just smiling when the Vicar said her class, once unmanageable, was now the best-behaved of all.

She was *awful*. But our confidence in her goodness never wavered.

9

. . . NOR did the thought ever enter my head that the aunts—so exciting to look at and to be with, so gifted as it seemed to me, so different from other people's aunts—were really just lonely girls, clinging to our mother for warmth and reassurance in a changing world; that living in hostels or lodgings as they did, they had washed their hair and put on their best when they came to see us, pleased and even excited to visit us in our cottage to which I thought like princesses they condescended.

As the war dragged on, and there were food shortages and talk of the hundreds of thousands of young men being killed at the front, the aunts became thinner and thinner, more and more nervy, and more and more subject to hurt feelings and fits of tears. Sometimes the sisters would seem almost to burst from the cottage, to go for long walks along the lanes; disregarding lowering skies, snow and hail—eyes shining, teeth gleaming, joking and laughing, the wind tugging at hats and veils, and hail finding the hollows of clothing to gather there. In spring, when the hawthorn was thickly in flower and the air heavy with its scent, our mother might pause to gaze up at the masses of blossom, and drawing in great breaths, sing,

When the hawthorn blooms again,
Molly darling, I'll return;
And together we will wander down the lane
To the same old rustic dell,
Which we learned to love so well;
In the springtime,
When the hawthorn blooms again.

'Come on, Amy,' the aunts would say, looking back over their shoulders.

Most of the song sheets our mother bought then had the same theme:

When you come home, dear, when you come home;
No more to wander, no more to roam;
God will remember, He will provide
When you come home at eventide . . .

and

When the great red dawn is shining,
When the waiting hours are past;
When the tears of night are ended,
And I see the day at last;
I shall come down a road of sunshine
To a heart that is fond and true;
When the great red dawn is shining . . .

She sang them all; not particularly sadly, and certainly not soulfully, but confidently, with enjoyment.

*　　　*　　　*

During the Christmas which was to be the last before the war ended, it really did seem as if it were colder inside the cottage than out of doors, with a dead, damp, hopeless kind of cold which piling fuel on to the fire could not assuage. Across the lane the snow had drifted as high as the hedge, and the trees, shrouded for most of the day in mist, were stiffly encrusted with frost. The draughts under the doors were the icy breath of the north wind.

When Aunt Winifred and Aunt Kate had arrived two days before, I had been unable to greet them, being immobilized by toothache and a sore throat; sitting on a chair, knees drawn up to chin and arms tightly round legs, exercising will-power. Imprudently, I had spent almost all the day before lying beneath the mahogany table reading, bare knees resting on the green carpet with its distinctive mushroomy smell, and bent head in full range of the half-inch gap at the bottom of the front door.

In spite of looking wan and thin, the aunts were bright, and bent on keeping up the spirit of Christmas. They had brought presents and a box of Christmas crackers.

With Christmas Day came falling snow, and so deep did it lie that to go to church was out of the question and we settled down to a day indoors. Our landlord had sent us the traditional gift of beef, bright red and dripping with blood, and our mother put everything she could muster into the Christmas dinner. The small deal table, with its starched white cloth, was crammed with plates, knives and forks, spoons, gravy, Yorkshire pudding, roast potatoes, sprouts, and the beef. We pulled our crackers, read our mottoes, and donned our paper hats.

'Have some more gravy, Winnie,' my mother said, beaming proudly, 'have some more; do have some, there's plenty.' She pushed the gravy-boat towards Aunt Winifred, but it tripped on the crowded table and somehow, to everyone's horror, a puddle of gravy appeared in the lap of the new, long, green velvet dress which was Aunt Winifred's contribution to the sense of occasion.

Aunt Winifred turned irritably upon our mother, but my sister intervened. 'It wasn't her fault,' she pronounced calmly, 'it was your fault for moving the plate.'

At this, Aunt Winifred burst into tears, and mopping at her dress with a table-napkin with one hand, and pressing her handkerchief to her mouth with the other, she extracted herself from her place at the table round which we were packed tight as sardines.

'You let them be as rude as they like to me,' she sobbed. 'You never keep them under control; they can say anything they like to me.' And she retreated upstairs to our mother's bedroom where, directly overhead, we soon heard creaks and muffled weeping.

As always at such times, Aunt Kate preserved a tactful silence, and our mother, guardian of the congenuity and the spirit of Christmas, rallied her powers to meet the emergency.

'Leave her,' she said. 'She looks very run down; it will do her good to have a weep.' She turned to my sister. '. . . and then you'd better go up and apologize.'

'I haven't done anything wrong,' said my sister. 'I'm not going to apologize when I haven't done anything wrong. I was only sticking up for you.'

Our mother looked thoughtful. Not always in a clash of wills with my sister could she be certain of maintaining the upper hand. She turned to me.

'You must go and apologize, then.'

'*Me?* I didn't do anything wrong either.'

But our mother was on safer ground here, and knew it. 'You laughed,' she said firmly.

Laughed?

Going to the corner where the coats were hung, she produced my father's walking-stick. She had never hit us in our lives, but now she brandished the stick as if to the manner born.

'Up you go now,' she said, 'and no nonsense.' And driving me before her as if I were a cow or a calf, she conducted me, now sniffing and sobbing, into the other room and up the stairs.

Thus we emerged into my mother's bedroom, to find

Aunt Winifred sitting near the dressing-table, still crying, and in a very tragic pose. But it was not the sight of Aunt Winifred that arrested my attention and dried my tears. It was the reflection of my own face confronting me. It was true, just as Aunt Kate had always said. I *did* look like a kipper when I cried. There I was in the looking-glass . . . a kipper, wearing a blue paper crown.

The apology having been made, Aunt Winifred returned to the table, and our Christmas feast proceeded quite cheerfully, Aunt Winifred being almost bright now, and, to my surprise, especially kind to me.

The washing-up done, we all brushed our hair and moved into the other room, where a lively fire made dancing reflections in the polished furniture, without, however, having much effect upon the temperature of the damp, draughty little room. My sister and I could not wait for everyone to write in the autograph albums we had been given for Christmas.

> He whom love would seek, (wrote Aunt Kate)
> Let him love evermore,
> But seldom speak.
> For in love's domain
> Silence must reign;
> Lest it bring to the heart
> Grief and pain.

('Fancy Kitty writing that!' said our mother when, later, she saw it, her eyes bright and interested at this talk of love. 'Whatever could have made her write that, I wonder.')

Aunt Winifred wrote:

> O let the solid ground not fail beneath my feet,
> Before my life has found what some have found so sweet.
> Then let come what come may;
> What matter if I do go mad, I shall have had my day.

My mother wrote:

59

As old Mrs Terrier said to her pup,
'In all life's adversities,
Keep your tail up.'

After tea, as we sat at the lamplit table, drowsy and
replete, my mother said she would tell fortunes in the
teacups, and we leaned forward with our elbows on the
table to watch, as ceremoniously she accepted a cup and
took on her role. We were silent as with the cup in her left
hand she turned it three times from the left, then placed it
upside-down over the saucer, leaving it there while she
counted fifty.

'Have you wished?'

She turned the cup the right way up and examined the
remaining tea-leaves from all angles. Then, before she
could speak, ' "You will *get* your wish," ' we chorused.

'You will *get* your wish,' she said, ignoring us but with a
warm smile for her victim, dignity and authority unruffled.
She studied the tea-leaves again.

'What can you see? What is it?'

'A line of dots. Look, it really is there. It means a long
journey, and look, a *key*! Your circumstances will improve . . . and here, surely this is a flaming torch—*that*
means an unexpected piece of good fortune, or it *can* mean
the discovery of an undeveloped talent.'

We turned with new respect to the talented one who was
looking gratified, in spite of herself.

'. . . and this long tea-leaf, nearly at the top, it means that
you will soon be meeting a tall dark stranger . . . you can
laugh, but look, it really is there.'

Round the fire it was more convenient to read the palm.
'This is a very good life-line, you will live to be a hundred,'
our mother promised recklessly. 'Bend your hand . . . yes,
four children . . . and *this* is your line of happiness—see
how long and deep it is.'

To round off the evening and send the aunts warm to

bed, my mother now produced a bottle of plum wine which had been given to her by the old man who did the garden. It looked innocent enough, and after all it was home-made, so she and the aunts each drank a cupful. Not long after, however, they began to back away from the fire, saying how hot it was. 'Absolutely stifling!' gasped Aunt Winifred suddenly, clutching at her chest.

Then they began to take off their clothes. First frocks, then even petticoats. Finally, exclaiming at the strangeness of the weather, they opened the door to the cold and darkness, and sat on the doorstep. And gazing at the snow lying there in the heat, they were suddenly overcome by the funny side of it all, and began to laugh and laugh, tears pouring down their cheeks, while my sister and I stood watching, puzzled, and very, very disapproving.

* * * * *
* * * *
* * * * *

10

WHEN our father had come home from the war he had driven up looking like a king, in an open horse-drawn cab from the town, not Turnham's cart which was usually hired for visitors. We had all gone to London to stay for a week, having meals in restaurants and going to see *Charlie's Aunt* and *The Maid of the Mountains*. Such a way of life my sister and I had never known, and we thoroughly distrusted it. 'It's their own fault,' my sister said now, 'they shouldn't have been so extravagant when he came home.' She pursed her lips and her eyes were stern.

Evening after evening, dusty and dispirited, our father returned to the cottage from his searching for a house. It was our first taste of worry.

When our father worried the energy he generated was enormous. Waves of worry flowed from him—one could almost see it playing round his head like forked lightning, and it penetrated every corner of the cottage. As far as one could tell, our mother was not affected by his mood, but my sister and I soon succumbed, and crept out, each to her own pigsty, to worry too.

As we lay in bed after a day of pouring rain, we heard our parents talking in the room below.

'You'd have been better off if I'd never come back,' our father rumbled, 'at least you'd have had a pension and you wouldn't have been turned out.'

Then our mother's higher, lighter voice. 'That's just silly talk. It's only for the time being.'

At last, when it seemed the searching and waiting would never end, our father came across a small derelict shop, squeezed between a chemist's and jeweller's in the Market Square of a nearby town; derelict because the owners could not afford to make the premises habitable. Overjoyed by his find, he was undeterred by the dilapidation and dirt and the protests of the owners; it was a house and it was empty, and he was prepared to fight for it.

'My wife and I have only thirty pounds in the world, but if you will let us rent it I will undertake to spend half of that money on doing it up.' As always, his imagination leaped ahead. 'My wife might have a little business of some kind, and we should soon put the place on its feet.'

Impressed by his enthusiasm, the landlords not only agreed to let, but offered to help with the repairs.

The Rich Mrs Robinson

As our mother stood, for the first time, in the small dark room which was to be the shop, she looked round in dismay. It had been empty, we were told, a good while.

The last tenant had been a cobbler. His old backless chair, surrounded by leather trimmings, still stood in the middle of a floor which in places was inches deep in dirt and rubbish. Year by year the dust and cobwebs must have encroached, and mice and rats had their way. In one place the floorboards seemed to have disintegrated, disclosing what looked like bare earth, and in spite of the tenantless state of the little shop, its atmosphere was airless and stale. The walls were covered by dirty peeling paper. Here and there a ragged advertisement survived, tacked to the wall—'Woodmilne Rubber Heels', 'Cherry Blossom', and surprisingly, 'Mazawattee Tea'. The ceiling was yellowed and fly-blown, and the panes of glass in the shop-window so thick with cobwebs and grime that it was impossible to distinguish passers-by in the world outside.

The chemist from next door, a middle-aged widow, minded the key and was showing us round. 'You see I shall do away with the passage from the shop door, by taking down this partition,' our father was saying, giving the partition an affectionate pat, 'and with the wood, I shall make a counter, and a platform at the window which will have a white curtain round it on a brass rail.'

Our mother said nothing; full of ideas he might be, but he was no carpenter.

'*Here*'—he waved an arm—'I shall make fixtures for the

63

stock. Your counter will be *here.*' We listened disbeliev-
ingly, discouragement oozing from every pore, and again
our mother said nothing.

She was silent, too, when the chemist showed us over the
rest of the house: a small living-room behind the shop,
leading into a kitchen, where we saw a rusty stove piled
with soot and lumps of cement, a larder with fungus-
covered walls, a copper, an old stone sink, a pump, and a
floor of tiles chipped and stained. The kitchen had an
offensive smell, and after a quick glance round, our father
closed the door.

Unexpectedly, there were four good bedrooms. In his
heyday the chemist's predecessor had expanded his business into our shop premises, but had taken no part of the
upper rooms. 'This front bedroom would make a very nice
sitting-room,' suggested our guide encouragingly, as our
mother gazed down into the Square, 'a very nice outlook.'

At the back of the house was a wedge-shaped length of
trampled earth: the garden which we were to share with the
chemist, whose own shop frontage had access through a
long, narrow, cobbled passageway. This garden was
bounded irregularly on one side by a brick wall of varying
height, which confined a tangle of gardens, sheds, and
privies—the back premises of the shops and houses which
merged from the Square, round the corner, and into the
High Street; the other side was bounded by the backs of
cowsheds belonging to a farm. The far end was occupied
by a chicken-house, complete with chickens, which
belonged to the chemist, and a coal pile. There were several
well-established bonfire sites, a heap of scrap-iron, and
outcrops of a strange plant, identified by the chemist as
balsam.

Our father's enthusiasm remained undimmed, burning
bright and eager, and three months later, with the help of
workmen, the shop, at least, was dirty no longer. Through-

out was a pleasant smell of new wood and varnish, and as well as cleanliness, a certain daintiness: our mother liked things to be just so, and not, as she would grumble to our father, 'all piggy'.

To the customer's right on entering was the shop-counter; that counter which our father's mind's eye had seen and his single-minded struggles with the wooden partition achieved. Two doors led to the living-room, one on the customer's side and the other in the corner behind the counter. In the space on the customer's side, perhaps a yard in width, was laid a strip of brown linoleum with key-pattern edging. There was a similar space behind the counter, and then, against the wall, the fixtures waiting for stock.

At the window was a platform about a foot in height and a yard in depth, the window-space thus formed being separated from the body of the shop by a crisp white curtain hanging from a brass rail. It was the platform and the curtain seen by our father in his vision; nevertheless, I was inclined to agree with my sister's pronouncement that ours did not really look like a proper shop. In any case it seemed strange to me that we should be having a shop at all—almost as if it were some game our parents were playing.

The living quarters were not yet finished, although most of the rooms had been decorated. The upstairs front room which the chemist had suggested as a sitting-room was complete, with the carpet laid, and Herodias, Lady Townsend, and the monkey lawyers in possession, but repeated attempts to get the mahogany table and the piano up the stairs or through the window having failed, they were left in the room behind the shop. Our father had spent hours scraping, scrubbing, and painting in the kitchen; and we soon learned the ways of the pump—a clanking monster encased in wood—always remembering to keep water saved for pouring in at the top to make it suck up, and to work its long, limply-hanging arm gently in case a jet of water should suddenly shoot out, missing the sink altogether.

Already, to us, the house was beginning to look homely, with fresh new curtains, and flowers from the railway embankment where my sister and I played with the children from next door—many familiar flowers were there, moon daisies, dog-roses, pink clover, sorrel... With our new friends we slid down the handrail at the crossing, and sometimes when it was getting dark went with them into the sewerage nearby, to take flying leaps over the network of ditches in the waning light.

Our father had found temporary work with a coal merchant, John J. Marshall, who was trying to establish a business in the neighbouring town. Sometimes in the cool of the evening our father and mother would stroll up and down the narrow length of garden, while I gambolled round them in bedroom slippers, and my sister practised scales. Over the cowsheds the sky was pink, and I could see the spire of the church and the tops of trees. Then I almost forgot the cottage.

✻   ✻   ✻

And now it was three o'clock on a drowsy summer afternoon. That morning a notice had appeared in the shop-window, printed in our father's bold artistic hand, to say that we were 'OPEN'.

It seemed to me to be a day of very great importance, and for some reason it seemed vital that I should be present when the first customer came in; so much so that I had been sitting beneath the counter for most of the day, even eating my dinner there. But to our embarrassed surprise, the shop-bell had not rung, no one had come in. Now in the stillness and heat of the afternoon the town seemed to be resting. Just occasionally I heard echoing footsteps pass along the pavement, but they passed, no one stopped at our door.

Before me, as I sat in my hiding place, were the fixtures, waiting for stock; and there to my right was the curtain hanging from its brass rail. Rising above and beyond the curtain could be seen the top of a blue dress. It was mine. Aunt Kate had sent a length of silk from abroad where, having married a rich man, she now lived, and part of this material my mother had been making up for my birthday; and there was my frock, taking pride of place in the centre of the shop-window, raised on a stand our father had made from a coat-hanger, a brass stair-rod, and an ingeniously built-up wooden plinth. With two-inch black velvet ribbon slotted round the waist, and embroidered with a true-lover's knot on the chest, and scallops and French knots round the collar, my frock was quite a bargain at 15s. 6d.

My sister had contributed to the stock a cherished box of handkerchiefs, and from our mother's drawer had come an unused pair of kid gloves, a present from Aunt Winifred. An account had been opened at one of the wholesale warehouses in Cheapside, and two dozen heather-mixture stockings, to sell at one-and-eleven-three, and six voile blouses at twelve-and-eleven-three, had been bought. The stockings were fashionable just then, thick in texture—a mixture of wool and lisle—seamless, and of a purplish colour. The blouses, flowered and frilly, would, according to our father, sell like hot cakes.

Although our mother had delighted in dressing the window, and although the window itself was so small, it had been difficult to dispose our goods to advantage and in such a way as to dispel a suggestion of frugality. As for the fixtures to hold stock, the discarded blouse-boxes had been piled there at first but had looked so lost that it was considered the general effect would be better, perhaps, without them. A blouse had been placed on a small stand at one end of the counter, and several pairs of stockings strewn negligently at the other end, but although the window was endowed with all the rest of the stock, it still looked to us a little unnatural, a little bare.

'But it's better than having it overcrowded,' our mother, eyeing it, said at last, 'better taste. Better class shops never do have much in the window. Some of the very best shops have just one thing—flung.' Her gesture hinted at the careless perfection of that fling.

I had been sitting in my house beneath the counter for so long that I had become drowsy, and when at last I heard the sound I had been waiting to hear I could hardly believe it; but there was no doubt that the door had opened, the bell had rung, and *someone had come into our shop!*

Almost at once our mother appeared through the door at the back, and without glancing in my direction came forward; placing her hands lightly on the edge of the counter above me, she smiled at whoever was on the other side.

It was as if a game had come to life: a customer, a real customer, was in our shop! and my head rose above the edge of the counter.

What I saw was not someone in a big hat with cherries round it, and kid gloves, it was an old, old woman in a battered felt hat from which white hair strayed. She had a cast in one eye and seemed to have only one tooth, and wore a sagging black cardigan and a black apron. She had brought into the shop a washing-basket, and this she now set upon the floor.

'D'ye sell black cotton?'

Black cotton, and we hadn't any cotton. But my mother was equal to the occasion and did not hesitate. Her smile was all confidence, warmth, and encouragement.

'I shall be having some in,' she said, 'perhaps you will be coming in again some time.'

But the old woman did not move. Her gaze wandered slowly round the shop, coming to rest on the heather-mixture stockings on the counter. She pushed a gnarled hand into the top of a stocking, considering its texture between finger and thumb.

'How much?'

'One-and-eleven-three,' said our mother.

The old woman lifted her apron, then her skirt, rummaged in a pocket, brought out a purse, and for a long time surveyed its contents.

'Well, I b'ain't got it.'

'You could bring the rest another day,' said my mother.

The stockings wrapped, and the customer gone, my sister came in, and together we watched our mother take two books from a ledge beneath the counter. Opening one, she smoothed the first clean empty page, and wrote at the top, 'August 17th, 1920', and then, 'Stockings . . . . . . 1s. 11¾d.' Then she opened the other book and wrote, 'August 17th, 1920. Mrs Washing-Basket to pay on stockings . . . . . . 9d.' Blotting the entries carefully, she studied them for a moment, then closed the books and put them away.

'Daddy says we shall go broke,' I said. 'He says we shall all end in the workhouse.' I did not know exactly what going broke was, but I knew what it meant to me. It meant that we should be 'poor people', and the deep nightmare fear that we might have to be poor people in London.

'Don't take any notice of him; you know what he is, the old Gummidge.'

She opened the battered tin cash-box which was serving as a till, took two pennies from the money so lately deposited there, and gave my sister and me one each. 'Go and buy yourselves a little treat.' Satisfied, I took my penny, and with my sister went out into the Square.

✳   ✳   ✳

The Square, with its arched Market House, was small and intimate, the centre of a town which was little more than a village; indeed we were to notice that some of the new people, businessmen and others, who soon came to live on the outskirts, were to call it 'the village', whether in belittlement, or to stress the rusticity of their environment, it would be difficult to say.

The town's three main streets converged upon the Square, and a lane led away in the direction of some old lime trees. Beyond, rose the tall grey spire of the church, delicate and withdrawn.

There was a disused malt-house, and in the Square a red-brick archway supporting a red lion led to a weed-grown cobbled yard and a tall chimney-stack, still called the Brewery, although fallen into decay.

Over all the town was a curious air of dilapidation. In the High Street itself were some sagging roofs, and thatched cottages reputed still to have earth floors.

We were to find that the green rising ground visible over the roofs at the top of the High Street could be yellow with buttercups and cowslips and dotted with grazing cows; and that in early summer there would always come a day, which filled our mother with delight, when a favourable breeze brought to the Square and to the High Street an invasion of white seed-fluff from a group of willow trees growing somewhere in the direction of the church. 'Look,' our mother would say, 'it's come; it's snowing!'

A wit from Bishopstone had stayed here for a night and had reported the town to be so quiet that he had been unable to sleep. Children played marbles in the High Street and whipped their tops round and round the Market House.

Very few of the shops had plate-glass windows, seeming more like houses used as shops than real shops to my sister and me. The tailor, with his black skull-cap and long white beard, sat cross-legged in his shop-window, sewing; the baker's shop had a heavy stable door and was approached by precipitous stone steps; in the jeweller's window was a selection of cheap brooches, pendants, and chains, 'Rolled Gold' and seemingly fixed permanently to fly-blown, yellowing card. Even our shop, we found later, was as much a proper shop as the shoe-shop in the High Street. There, if one wanted to buy a pair of shoes, one went to the butcher's a few doors further on. The butcher, fat and solemn, would call his wife, remove his apron, take a key down from the wall, and precede the customer slowly and with dignity to the shoe-shop, where he would unlock the door. One could see then that this shop was rather dusty; moreover the piles of shoe-boxes were crooked, and some boxes had lost their lids. Usually, after a prolonged search, it was found that the shoes desired were not in stock, and a well-thumbed catalogue would be consulted at some length, and the shoes ordered.

At the sweet-shop the owner, Mrs Wilkins, presided. She was very fat, but her shrewd old eyes were the eyes of a good woman of business. Her counter was covered with open boxes of sweets—pear drops, cupid favours, wine gums, dolly mixture—Mrs Wilkins's speciality was 'two penn'orth o'mixed'; sometimes when she was serving a child from a poor family her hand would dip liberally into one box after another until there would be more than half a pound of sweets, but Mrs Wilkins was her own mistress and that was her affair.

She accepted my offer to pass her the bottle of raspberry

drops which was on one of the shelves on our side of the counter.

' "A little help is worth a deal of pity."No, not like that, you'll drop it. Just put your fingers under the jar and work it into your hand, then hold it steady with the other. That's right.'

There was not much that Mrs Wilkins did not know about what went on in the town, and in the High Street and the Square especially.

'Your father got a job yet?'

We told her about John J. Marshall.

'Coal-heaving, eh!' She tore a paper bag from a bundle suspended from a nail, and blowing it open, shot the sweets in. 'Your mother doesn't sell corsets, I suppose?'.

Corsets! But then shops did sell corsets. Perhaps we should be having some in, and I gazed in fascination at Mrs Wilkins's billowing rolls. Was it possible for corsets to be quite as big? Whatever would they look like off? And even more amazing, whatever would they look like on?

'Perhaps my mother could come and measure you and have some specially made,' said my sister seriously, going straight to the point.

'I should be much obliged if she would.'

My sister and Mrs Wilkins had exchanged roles. Mrs Wilkins had become the customer and, almost humbly it seemed, was seeking advice. My sister had become the shopkeeper, the expert. Leaning forward, Mrs Wilkins lowered her voice.

'I've been getting a little stout since George (my husband) went. I need support. I've been at my wits' end! Here I am, tied hand and foot to the business, and do you think I can get anyone to find anything that fits me?' She gazed mournfully into my sister's youthful eyes and shook her head.

Out in the street we waited before crossing, while a herd

of cows with full swinging udders went leisurely past on its way to the farm; and when we reached the Square a crocodile of girls passed by, the Home girls, from the church orphanage, who were on their way back from school. Two by two and hand in hand, unescorted, they made their decorous way, the smaller ones in front and the older ones behind. They wore hard, white straw boater hats, green cotton frocks with white tuckers, print pinafores, black, hand-knitted woollen stockings, and black leather boots. They set a standard of respectable austerity at the school my sister and I were soon to attend, making up almost half of the pupils there.

※   ※   ※

Once we had started school the days fell into their allotted places. The town began to open to us on every side, the shop introducing us, and pressing us forcibly into all kinds of new activity.

A small stream of customers began to come into our shop. Some evidently came out of curiosity, or out of kindness to give us a start; others because there had been need of a new shop. Almost every customer, however, seemed to have her own sphere of interest in the town, and there seemed an unspoken obligation for our mother, receiving patronage, to support each one. Soon the shop-window was to carry posters advertising rummage sales, revivals, fêtes, dances, and whist-drives. Nearer Christmas, books of raffle tickets would appear on the counter, sometimes even the prizes themselves: iced cakes, dressed dolls, and baskets of fruit—there seemed no limit to the customers' activity. As the weeks went by my sister and I also, having long hair and good voices, were to be pressed into use in a variety of roles:

> We are the Summer Fairies,
> Bringing the Golden Hours . . .

73

We are the Thieves,
The forty Thieves . . .

Onward tread, ye soldiers of the right,
Know no dread to put the foe to flight . . .

We joined the Band of Hope, swearing to abstain from alcoholic liquor so long as we should remain members. We were to help, with innocent treachery, the Conservatives and the Liberals without discrimination.

On Tuesday evenings we went to dancing classes just started by two of the customers. The charge was sixpence

'We are the Summer Fairies'

each, and we learned the waltz, the barn dance, the two-step, and the lancers. My sister attended to her own toilet, but to be on the safe side our mother gave me a good hot wash before brushing my hair and attiring me in what our father, amusedly watching preparations over the top of his newspaper, called my 'snotty-goggle frock', because of a large spray of what appeared to be yew berries embroidered on the front. I felt very foolish in this dress, which had a wide frill, Bubbles fashion, round the neck,

74

but both my sister and I were used to our mother's artistic adventures in the way of dresses made from odd pieces of material or from aunts' old dresses, and resigned ourselves. My sister was in green velvet with a girdle of wooden beads, and there was magic in the air, as if we were going to a ball.

Our life at the cottage seemed very far away. Because of the roofs of the houses, the sky seemed to have shrunk, and our journeyings to and from school were no longer battles with the wind and the rain, but a hurried scramble of a hundred yards or so. We were becoming quite used to our new life and to the idea that our mother should spend so much of her time behind the counter.

Sometimes when we came home from school a customer would be standing on the kitchen table, while our mother, her mouth full of pins, knelt on the floor adjusting the hem of a frock. She never relinquished a possible sale without a struggle, altering, almost remaking dresses to get them to fit, encouraging faint-hearted customers.

'I could let the seam out each side, and swathe round a piece of Liberty silk I have by me,' she would say, standing back and viewing the customer with a professional air.

Now, when she was asked for something not in stock, she would say, 'I am expecting some in any day; one of my little girls will bring it round.' Then she would call us into the shop, introducing us with pride, however untidy we happened to be; and when the customer had gone, write out an order, which we would take to catch the next post.

She was never bothered by children, and I often stood by her as she served in the shop, the customers disregarding me completely, almost as if I were invisible, and continuing with their confidences.

'He treated me *terribly*, right from the start . . .'

And, to my puzzlement, on another occasion the same

customer: 'Those first eight years of my marriage were the happiest days of my life!'

Our mother never 'repeated things', even in the bosom of the family, nor did she say much when customers told her their troubles; just a small sympathetic noise now and then, or perhaps sometimes she would blink a little, or I might notice her surreptitiously taking the ticket off what the customer was buying, or marking it down.

She was getting more orders for needlework now, blouses and dresses and loose covers. Often my sister and I would have the miserable job of standing in for other children's fittings, our mother cheering us on with 'Only

'Only another minute, duckie'

another minute, duckie; just walk over there once more . . . now turn round . . . walk over towards the door again . . . come here. Yes, that's better, that's right.' She smiled her lovely smile, but in vain; we stood shivering and complaining, jumping and fussing every time she stuck a pin into us. It was bad enough being fitted for our own things, without having to do it for other children.

Soon the fixtures behind the counter began to fill with boxes and packets. We were also beginning to stock one or two coats. Our father had managed to get a second-hand till in place of the old cash box. Ours really was beginning to look like a proper shop.

＊   ＊   ＊

At this time, something was taking place which was to have far-reaching consequences for the town, and in particular for those men who, like our father, had recently been demobilized. Five chairmakers had begun work in a small, disused school. They worked from half-past seven in the morning until six in the evening when orders were forthcoming, and were paid a shilling an hour. For an urgent order the men would go in at four in the morning, working by candlelight: the order having been completed by noon, there might be no more activity for the rest of the week. There was a rumour that with sufficient orders, men who brought their own tools with them might be taken on and paid ten shillings a week, and piece-work prices on every chair they stood up. It was a chair-making district, where for generations chair-bodgers had worked in clearings among the beech trees in the surrounding woods. Local people had already begun to call the school 'the Chair Factory'.

※　　　※　　　※

I had been surprised that the chemist should have thought the view from our upstairs sitting-room 'a very nice outlook', but we saw much of what was going on in the town from its windows: a procession, perhaps, headed by a band and men in bowler hats carrying a picture banner with cords and tassels, the Friendly Societies of the town collecting for the hospital; the horse-drawn fire-engine driving into the Square for the firemen, some with long white beards, to test the apparatus. One day we found that the pavements all up the High Street were lined with vegetables—the entries for the Agricultural Show. Each summer, a group of Scouts camped in the White Lion meadow at the top of the High Street, and every evening, in that short, quiet time which comes to villages and small towns when the workers return, a shrill, unfamiliar sound hung on the air, becoming louder, and accompanied by singing, as the boys marched down the High Street preceded by a fife band. Hats well tilted, pale sinewy knees straining manfully to the long strides, they spread their ranks across the street almost pavement to pavement, and as they approached, the words of their song became clearer:

> We are some of the East Ham boys,
> We are the East Ham boys.
> We know our manners,
> We spend our tanners,
> We are respected wherever we go . . .

Round the Square they wheeled and then, again extending their ranks, retired back up the High Street and to their tents.

Delivering parcels soon made my sister and me familiar with the town and its outskirts—the shops, the handsome old houses in the High Street, the little flint cottages with their neat squares of garden, the Victorian villas, and the farms.

It was I who had taken Mrs Wilkins's corsets over when at last the parcel arrived. They had been a long time coming, but had we only known it, their arrival was to make the day one of some importance.

Mrs Wilkins was serving a customer when I manoeuvred through the door, but her eyes brightened. She winked.

'That'll be my . . . I expect,' she said, and when the customer had gone, 'Just you wait here a minute in case someone comes in. I want to try them on.'

She disappeared into the back room, and I sat down on a crate of ginger beer to wait. She was gone for quite a long time; then the door opened and she emerged. Standing behind the counter, she rotated slowly for my inspection. 'What d'you think of me then?' she asked eagerly.

She, evidently, was delighted; she glowed with satisfaction. 'And I wouldn't know I had them on! I haven't been able to wear this frock for years. You can tell your mother I'm very, very pleased. *Very* pleased.' She really did look several sizes smaller—almost trim in a majestic kind of way.

'She's sent the bill, I see. I'll pay right away. I expect she'll be glad of the money.' Turning her back to me, and pulling up her skirts, she rummaged awhile in the region of

'the handsome old houses in the High Street'

her knees. Turning with a wallet in her hand she counted some notes from an amazing bundle and put them into the envelope with the bill.

'You tell your mother she's done me a real good turn.' She reached up and took a box of chocolates from one of the shelves, and put it into a paper bag.

'Here, you give her these King George's and tell her I'm very grateful. She's a wonderful woman your mother is.'

No advertising campaign could have been more effective than Mrs Wilkins's expressions of gratitude and pleasure oft repeated to her customers; full-page advertisements in all the national papers could hardly have drawn the attention of the town to our shop more completely than she. There was a definite increase in trade. Our mother was now accepted as an expert in the realm of fittings, and her name was known in every part of the town. There began what was to become quite a brisk trade in 'specials'; not only corsets but complete outfits for weddings and other functions. Customers who were worried about finding 'something really nice, and *right*' for a special occasion, were often glad to hand over this responsibility to our mother. She would take endless trouble, and began to get quite a reputation. Now when she was asked for something not in stock, she would say, 'I will look for something special when I go to Town.'

In this way even our school lives were to become influenced by the shop. Ours was 'the best attending school in the county'. Before we had come weeks, even months, were known to go by without a single absence. An absent child was not spoken of as 'away' or 'ill', but in awed tones and with shocked faces, '*He has broken the hundred per cent!*'

In winter there was almost always a child or two sitting limply by the fire-guard. Work was not required of them; they were the heroes, who rather than be absent, had come, in spite of illness, bringing their medicine bottles with them. At prize-giving, certificates were given for good attendance, and seals each year to renew them . . . 'Harold Tidmarsh, three years never absent, never late; Samuel Parker, three years never absent, never late; Nora Tompkins FIVE years (clapping) never absent, never late . . . '

Eager to please as my sister was, she was doomed never to be included in this roll of honour; each half-closing day that our mother went to London, she boldly took the morning off from school. In fact, nothing was ever said about her defection; everyone knew she was minding the shop; everyone also knew that dignified, conscientious, and able, she was the headmaster's pet.

Fears for our mother's safety (how could she possibly find her way in London without getting run over or lost?), my sister's truancy, and cold dinner, made Wednesday a bad day.

Monday, washing day, was unfavourable also, with steam from the copper, draughts from the back garden where the clothes were hung, the smell of wet wool, and the all-pervading dampness. And our mother, a little dishevelled for once, and red in the face, hurriedly serving boiled rice, with pallid, crinkled, washerwoman's hands.

Saturday was even worse, because it was on Saturday afternoons that our father did the bills.

First he sorted the invoices and put them into piles according to name all over the table, if necessary using also the floor on either side of his chair. Then, with much contrivance, he would decide which bills could be paid, bearing in mind the firms most likely to press us or cut off supplies, and the firms who supplied goods we needed urgently or could not do without.

As he sat, his face puckered with worry and the grumblings of his duodenal ulcer (his 'broken glass' as he called it), one of us would open the door from the kitchen or the door from the shop, and a strong draught would take the bills fluttering on to the wrong piles. There would be pandemonium. Then, muttering and growling, he would leave his chair, re-sort the bills, put them back on to the right piles—and then the shop-bell would ring, our mother would open the kitchen door, pass through, open the door to the shop, and again there would be a wild swirling of papers.

To keep the peace, and to save him from worrying too much, our mother would often hold back some of the bills, hiding them in the bottom of the till in the shop until such time as she had had a specially good day to soften the blow.

'Have I got them all now?'

'Of course.'

'*All?*'

And when he had squeezed out of her almost all of them, we would hear him groan aloud, 'Good Lord! Good Lord! Whatever's the woman thinking about. We shall go broke! We shall all end in the workhouse!'

At the end of the month he made out the customers' bills. 'Who the devil's this?' he would roar, ' "Mrs Sore Eyes"? and these, "Mrs Finger-to-her-Nose", "Mrs Five-children", Mrs Husband-going-abroad", "Mrs Going-to-do-her-Graves"; and *where the devil do they all live?*'

'We shall go broke!'

'I shall put a note at the bottom of this account,' he would bluff in desperation, writing out once more a bill long overdue. 'We're nearly on the rocks, woman. How can I pay the bills if you won't let me get the money in? Do they think we're bankers?'

But our mother, whose sense of delicacy would not permit her even to ask her customers' names or where they lived if these details were not offered when credit was required, could not bear the thought that they should feel humiliated, or should get into trouble from their husbands by threatened proceedings.

It really did seem just then as if everyone was 'going broke', and that year the Horticultural Society could not afford to hold its Annual Show. In the school building condemned before the war but still in use, children shared battered readers. There was little talk of going away for holidays, and a whole family ill with whooping cough, measles, or mumps, might not be considered sufficient cause for the expense of calling in the doctor. It was said that at the chair factory funds had been so short one week that there had not been enough money to pay the wages.

Nevertheless, our mother found that most of the ordinary people paid up; if not in cash, in kind: a sack of potatoes, some pears, plums, a chicken, eggs, honey, or a piece of pork. It was more often people considered to be well-off who ran up the heavy bills which were such a worry and which to a large extent nullified the progress being made in the shop. Their names were household words to us, although it must be admitted that customers who were not good payers were occasionally encouraged into indiscretions of buying by our mother herself, who became as carried away as they did if a dress suited them.

'Isn't that coat nice,' she said one day to an impecunious but clothes-loving customer.

'Yes, *isn't* it smart! If only I could afford to buy it. Oh, it would make me feel so *different* to have a new coat.'

'Me, too.'

There was a pause; then our mother said, 'Perhaps we could buy it between us and share it. I really only go out when I go to Town; you could wear it the rest of the time.'

❊   ❊   ❊

A worse worry even than the bills was Travellers. My sister and I lived in dread of them: Travellers our mother thought looked hungry; thin Travellers who reminded her of our father; Travellers with six children to clothe and feed; and Travellers who had booked no orders for a week. Also, it must be said, Travellers with beautiful samples, which she saw at a glance would suit such-and-such a customer so nicely.

'Haven't they anything more expensive,' our father would groan when he saw the bills, 'for the rich Mrs Robinson to order?'

She found it hard to be niggardly.

'You're so *wholesale*,' complained our father, 'they must think we're *shippers*.'

Sometimes my sister or I, in an agony of worry, would go and stand beside her when Travellers came, trying by baleful glances to crush them, as happily they spread their samples on the counter to snare our mother into bankruptcy.

'That will be all the big things this time,' she was telling a Traveller one day, 'but I have been asked for pearl buttons.'

The Traveller stood ready with his order book while she looked at the samples. 'How many, Madam?' and 'This is a very popular line.'

'Six,' I muttered gruffly, pulling at her skirt.

An indulgent glance passed between them.

'A gross, please,' she ordered with an air.

We came home from school at dinner-time one day to find a Traveller in the shop. He was leaning over the counter talking earnestly to our mother, and her eyes were full of tears. I saw a large tear beginning to run down her cheek, following the line of her nose. '. . . and then,' the Traveller was saying in a husky voice, 'she died in my arms!'

My sister and I exchanged glances.

Inside we found a strong smell of burnt potatoes. 'You lay the table, and I'll have a look at the dinner,' said my sister.

Soon everything was ready, but still we heard the murmur of voices. The minutes ticked by . . . five, ten, fifteen . . . half an hour, and still the voices went on.

'We shall be late!' wailed my sister, wringing her hands, 'I know we shall be late!' For the hundredth time she peered through the little curtained window into the shop.

'. . . and all the time she's ordering! . . . Oh dear! Oh

dear! I think I'd better go and cough.' Taking her place at the window, I watched her compose herself and go and stand beside our mother; then she lifted her hand to her mouth and gave a prim little cough.

Soon afterwards the Traveller concluded his ill-fated visit and left, first shaking our mother's hand with great warmth. 'It's very sad,' she said apologetically, hastily serving us with helpings of burnt potatoes, 'his mother has just died. I had to give him a little order.'

Not long after the Traveller's visit, it happened that the Square was becoming congested with wagons and lorries which had come to the town for the October fair; fresh contingents arrived daily, almost blocking the streets, encroaching on to the very pavements. There was a further excitement: we came out of school to find a young man distributing religious pamphlets and inviting us to a meeting in the meadow behind the High Street that evening. Fairmen were already assembling the giant round-about in the Square, and as I made my way up the High Street, with a small band of schoolfellows, to the meadow where the meeting was to be held, I saw that others had marked out their pitches and were unloading and erecting their tackle. It was getting cold, and the sun had set. In the meadow behind the High Street bare hedges and leafless trees were outlined against a vast luminous expanse of apricot and purest green. The wild, beautiful sky had been swept clean by a squally wind, and the clouds, black as soot, were piled far away. Looking up, I discovered a tiny silver star . . . and then another. It was the kind of sunset I was to associate ever afterwards with the October fair, and the sequel to the visit of the Traveller whose mother had, so unfortunately, died.

Although it was not yet dark, the evangelist had lighted a lantern. He was sitting on the steps of a caravan, playing a concertina, and a horse grazed nearby. Soon we had

overcome our shyness, and were standing grouped before
him while he taught us a song:

> I'm H.A.P.P.Y.,
> I'm H.A.P.P.Y.,
> I know I am, I'm sure I am,
> I'm H.A.P.P.Y.
>
> I'm S.A.V.E.D.,
> I'm S.A.V.E.D. . . .

But after a few more songs, and some prayers, and a little
talk, our eyes began to wander to the sky over the roofs of
the High Street, now inky as the sea, on which a bright
glare was beginning to spread. Sounds of music, too, began
to drift into our quiet meadow, the heart-warming
hurdy-gurdy of the roundabout. Our ears caught the crack
of coconut shies, and the shouting of voices, and soon the
young man dismissed us with another prayer, and a
pamphlet all round, and we ran off.

At the top of the High Street we halted, dazzled. The
street was lined with stalls and booths, each lit by a naked
flare. Celluloid balls danced in fountains of water waiting
to be shot down. Aunt Sally, a large, fat, shapeless rag doll
wearing a bonnet, waited to have the clay pipe bowled
from her mouth: 'Three turns for tuppence!' shouted the
showman, 'Three turns Aunt Sally!'

Another brawny-armed man was making mint hum-
bugs, throwing a skein of mixture like molten glass over a
hook fixed to his stall. Watched admiringly by a group of
children, he drew it out and looped it back again and again,
before cutting it into pieces with giant scissors and
arranging it on trays.

There were stalls with tubes of water for squirting down
necks, others selling bags of confetti or peppermint rock.
Swinging boats sailed high and low and a man in a tall
white chef's hat served fish and chips from a horse-drawn

kitchen. Rising over the head of the crowd was an enormous thermometer with a bell at the top where a man might try his strength with a sledge-hammer—now and then the bell would ring as some strong arm sent the indicator whizzing triumphantly to the top.

Men were shouting, and children darting between the booths screaming, squirting water down each other's necks, or throwing confetti. But above the din rose always the intoxicating wheezings of the giant roundabout, the heart and soul of the fair, which we could see down the length of the High Street. It shone in the Square like an immense birthday cake, its flashing lights glittering like diamonds.

Slowly we made our way down the street. There was Lily Dayton, who came to our school, with her brothers and sisters; each had a balloon, or a squirter, or a bag of chips, although at school they were looked upon as 'poor' children. The little girls of the family it was rumoured did not wear knickers; their neglected hair hung in their eyes and they smelled like coffee-grounds. When the nurse came to the school to look at heads she usually wrote something against their names in her book.

It seemed to me as if it were always 'poor' children who had toys; who had tops, skipping ropes, marbles, and transfers to stick on the backs of their hands. But I did not envy them, favouring the clannish austerity of the Home girls. These seldom brought toys or sweets to school, but if one of them did have a penny she might lay it out on slab dates, the stones being kept thriftily in a paper bag later to be lent out for sucking. Then, at playtime, she and her friends would walk about in groups, sucking impressively, 'swanking that they had some sweets'.

Arrived at the Square, we gazed up at the people riding on the roundabout. Gaily, godlike, they circled up there above our heads, carelessly astride their steeds. Up and down and round and round they went, among the flashing lights, the twinkling brass, the music, and the clashing cymbals of the plaster figures.

Behind the stalls our cobbled pavement was a quiet backwater. I opened the shop door. There, almost blocking my way, was a gigantic packing case. I squeezed past it. In the room behind the shop our father and mother sat at the table. To my horror I saw that our mother was crying. Our father had his arm round her. I had never seen her cry before.

I crept through into the kitchen. My sister was sitting hunched on a chair, the cat on her lap; she, too, was crying.

'What's happened? Is it that parcel?' I whispered, almost too shocked to speak. 'What's in it? How much was the bill?'

'It's veils, VEILS! . . . Fifteen pounds' worth! It was that Traveller whose mother died.'

She stared up at me. Her eyes were red and swollen with weeping. *'Fifteen pounds!'* she sobbed wildly. *'Fifteen pounds!* Wasted . . . because . . . because . . . n-n-nobody *wears* veils here, and *we* shan't be able to wear them . . .'

Quickly my mind ranged round the possibilities: our father . . . no, no; our mother . . . going to Town veiled, perhaps . . . but no; my sister and me . . . to Sunday school, to church, to dancing classes . . . curtains . . . It was no good, my sister was right. Nobody could wear them, and they were quite, quite useless.

Looking back, I am impressed that no one thought of returning the order.

Although the veils were to lie in the stock-room unpacked, our family was able to absorb almost all difficult stock. My sister and I went to school in stockings and bloomers which had been faded in the window so that one leg was a lighter shade than the other. We wore flawed stockings, and socks whose feet were of different sizes, and misfits of all kinds.

Our mother altered and wore dresses which had proved, after all, too advanced in style; and garments which had come up in the dyeing what she called 'a bad black'. Bad black was particularly abhorrent to her, and she would never never have offered for sale anything she considered as such.

Even our father wore ladies' expensive pure wool extra-outsize Wolsey vests, with V-neck, short sleeves, and capacious bust plackets, ordered by a customer who had then left the district.

'You're not to make him wear them,' my sister protested tearfully. 'Suppose he gets knocked down in the street, and they have to undress him. Whatever would people think of him!' Loyalty triumphed over modesty. 'It's those p-p-pockets,' she sobbed, 'those pockets for developments!'

'But he needs some winter vests badly.' Our mother gazed innocently into our father's eyes. 'They're a lovely quality, very strong: they'll last him for the rest of his life if he takes care of them.'

Only one thing found its way into the shop as a memorial of the Traveller whose mother had died: 'The Veil Lady', a plaster bust which the firm, delighted with what they must have thought an exceptionally promising market for veils, had sent for window display. She sat in the corner of our shop-window for a long time, wearing over her plaster hat a blue straw one trimmed with blue roses, which the chemist had bought at another shop, found she disliked, and asked our mother to try to sell for her.

I 2

THE first person up in the morning in our house had to unbolt the front door and put outside a jug with a saucer on top, for the milk, and coming down early one day I went straight into the shop. The shutters were up and the passageway was dim but I could still make out something which blocked my way to the door. It was the cat, lying dead, stiff and straight, a little pool of water by her mouth. Like other of the cats that came and went she must have taken poison the chemist had put down for the rats. If our mother saw the dead cat she would be sick, as she was so often now in the mornings—plaiting one of my pigtails, running off to be sick, then running back to do the second pigtail. The dead cat must be moved before our mother got up but I could not bring myself to touch it.

I stood and looked at it for quite a long time, my flesh creeping at the sight of the uncatlike posture—rather like a rabbit in a butcher's shop, I thought. I had once carried a rabbit home from the butcher's but I had not minded that.

Fetching a sheet of newspaper, I folded it small, and not without a shudder placed it round the outstretched back paws of the cat. Then I went to the back door and opened it ready and returned to where the cat lay. Pretending hard, I grasped the wrapped paws and picked up the body. It hung straight and stiff and heavy. It felt like a rabbit . . . a rabbit . . . a rabbit. I rushed out into the garden, right up to the end, where I laid my burden against the wall. My father would find it and bury it when he went to get in the coal. I shuddered. It was a *cat*! And I ran down the garden as fast as I could. Painstakingly I washed away all signs of the cat's death, and having completed that little task and put the jug out, I considered what I should do next. No one was stirring yet; I could see the Market House clock through the shop-window—ten-past six. I would get out our father's bike and have a ride round the Square till he was ready.

Precariously riding with one leg beneath the bar, I circled the Square, proudly, in the pure cool air of early morning. Few people were about. I could hear the milkman on his way, the noise of his hobnails sounding on the cobbled pavement as he went from house to house, and his buckets of milk clanking as he stood them down to measure out half a pint here, a pint there, into the waiting jugs. Now and then a small group of men would swish by on their bikes, and their voices would come ghostly back as they greeted others passing them further along the street.

'Watcher, Fred!'

'Mornin', George.'

Ten minutes still to seven o'clock; my father would be coming out soon, and now I noticed that someone was cycling behind me. I knew who it was: Muriel Simpkins. She was a pale girl, dressed in a neatly pleated grey skirt and a pink fluffy wool jumper. Her mouse-coloured hair hung down her back in one of the longest, thinnest pigtails I had ever seen; it tapered thinner and thinner till at the end, when almost invisible, it was tied with a large bow of wide, black, water-silk ribbon. She drew abreast and we circled the Square side by side.

'Why do you ride your father's bike?' Her voice came panting behind my ear. 'Where do you go to school? I go to Brackhurst Manor School in Kent. It's a school for ladies. You wouldn't be able to go, you're tradespeople.'

Then, 'I saw your sister yesterday. She's got a lot of hair, hasn't she. *My* hair is very fine. My mother's hair is fine, too. My mother is distantly related to the Queen.'

On the other side of the Square I could see my father

standing at the shop door, and with a skilful swerve I wobbled across.

'You should have been friendly to her, and spoken'—my sister was rather severe. 'Her mother bought a blouse the other day, she's quite a good customer. If you don't speak, and aren't friendly, customers won't come into our shop. You will be bad for trade.'

To some extent this was true. We were no longer free; we had to smile and not offend the customers. Customers, we found, gave or withheld their patronage for the strangest of reasons.

✻   ✻   ✻

It was on a Sunday morning that winter that the chemist called and took my sister and me for a walk. It turned out to be a very long walk indeed, and our father must have been looking out for us, because as we came home along the pavement he was standing at the door, waiting. He had an expression, a particular expression of pleasure, I had never seen on his face before, and to my amazement told us that we now had a little brother.

My sister and I were to stay to dinner and tea with the chemist, and when eventually we went home it was to find our mother's stepmother, Grandma Davies, in command. We were allowed upstairs to see our mother and the new baby. Our mother, as she lay in bed, drew her dressing-jacket closely round her.

'Daddy won't be able to say, "Three turns Aunt Sally!" any more, will he,' she said. I could see that she was telling us something, but I couldn't think what it was.

For a few days the house seemed thronged with people; there was Grandma Davies, and the district nurse, and even the doctor coming in. Then we were back in the old routine, except for our brother. He was not a very good baby, and cried nearly all the time.

'The doctor says it is lack of fats during the war years,' our mother said brightly when customers remarked.

During the winter evenings we would take it in turns to walk about the room nursing the baby, patting him rhythmically in time to a lullaby or a hymn. '*Yield* not to temptation,' we sang with heavy pats,

> *All* yielding is *si*-in,
> *Each* victory will *help* you
> *Some* other to *wi*-in . . .

Sometimes in the night we would wake to hear the floorboards creaking under our father, as he walked up and down, and we would hear him singing in a gruff muted voice,

> By-*by*ee, by-*by*,
> By-*by*ee, by-*by*,
> By-*by*ee, by-*by*ee,
> By-*by*ee, by-*by* . . .

His voice would tail off . . . stop altogether . . . There would be silence . . . silence . . . silence . . . Then a loud wail, and again the creak-creak and the 'By-*by*ee, by-*by*', as we turned over and drifted off again to sleep.

✳　　　✳　　　✳

'. . . and if a man or a woman comes up to you,' my father was saying seriously, 'and tells you, "Your mother has had an accident and has asked me to fetch you," don't take any notice. Just stay exactly where you are. Don't move whatever happens until your mother comes back.' I nodded, equally serious, but quite uncomprehending.

Our mother was going to London buying, for the first time since the baby was born, and as she was feeding him, he had to go too. I, for the first time, was to join my sister in the breaking of the hundred per cent. I was going to

London to hold the baby while our mother went to the warehouses in Cheapside. I was to sit in St Paul's churchyard and wait.

By half-past ten I was installed on a bench under the shadow of the cathedral, with an attaché case full of clean nappies beside me, and the baby in my arms. He was wearing his best gown, which reached almost to the ground when I stood up, and was wrapped in a white shawl. My hair was down for the occasion, instead of in the everyday plaits, and was tied with my best hair-ribbon.

Cautiously I began to eye my surroundings. There was quite a number of seats, but I saw no one sitting on them who seemed inclined to speak to me. In fact there was just one old man, sitting almost opposite me. He wore a shabby coat, very loose and long, and a ragged cap. He leaned forward on to his knees, muttering. Uneasily I turned my attention to the pigeons, which strutted about the path and between the old flat tombstones and the gnarled, stunted trees.

Above me rose St Paul's, its bulk incomprehensible—up, up to the dome and the gold cross. Beyond, I glimpsed the sky which also, I remembered, must be over our home, so far away.

Outside the big iron gates through which our mother had gone, a turmoil of traffic flowed. I saw the red tops of buses, and in the background the warehouses of Cheapside and St Paul's churchyard. We had passed the warehouses on our way, and I had noticed a brass plate whose words, 'Wholesale and Shipping', seemed familiar. At the iron gates my mother had turned to wave goodbye before disappearing into the traffic.

'I shan't be long,' she had said before she left us, 'be sure not to speak to anyone, won't you.'

Cautiously I looked over at the old man, but he seemed to have gone to sleep, and I set myself to wait.

A woman came through the gates and made her way along the path, disappearing round the side of the cathedral. At intervals, against the dull roar of the City, I heard a deep-throated bell telling the quarters. I had expected a long wait, and tried to put away the thought of what would happen and what I must do if my mother did not come back.

Again and again I looked towards the iron railings and the great iron gates, through which I could see the tangled mass outside. Might not our mother get run over trying to reach us? It seemed impossible that she, who could not do sums and was afraid of cows, could avoid it. My mind's eye saw her darting uncertainly among the traffic. Yes, she was almost sure to get run over. And if she was, how should I know? How would my father know? And what should I do? The baby might cry and refuse to be comforted. And then, if our mother *had* been run over, and someone came to tell me? . . . I knew even then I mustn't move. What danger was it that my father knew but I did not? 'If a man or a woman comes and says, "Your mother has had an accident and has asked me to fetch you." . . .'? But perhaps she really would have an accident and ask for me.

'*almost sure to get run over*'

The baby was unusually good, seeming drugged by the noise, and he liked being nursed, but he was getting rather heavy. Again I set myself to wait.

A boy, hatless, wearing a dark suit, and with red wrists, had come through the gates and seated himself nearby. He drew a packet of sandwiches from one pocket and a book from another, and settling himself comfortably began to munch and read. Then a man in a mackintosh and a bowler hat came, and gradually the seats around me began to fill, till the little churchyard was alive with a munching, reading throng. Now the seat of which I had been the sole occupant was a row of people; a man was sitting close to me, and then I must move the attaché case to make room for a boy.

Could I feel some of them staring at me?

I sat as still as possible and looked primly ahead. Then a voice was speaking. It was the man at my side. I gazed up in horror.

'Would you like a sandwich?' he asked kindly.

I looked at the sandwich. He had laid it on a crumpled paper bag and was offering it to me. Poisoned? Drugged! I look firmly ahead and said nothing.

Soon the man rose to his feet and walked away; but then on the other side of me a brown paper bag was offered.

''ave an apple.'

Blushing scarlet I made myself as small as possible and again said nothing. Then, as suddenly as it had come, the picnic party dispersed, and soon I was alone with the old man again, and the pigeons as they strutted about picking up the crumbs.

Now my worry became an ache. My back ached, too, and my arms, and my empty stomach. Now I was sure our mother had been run over, and it was just a question of sitting, and sitting . . . when I saw, coming through the gates, a familiar figure, and suddenly everything was all right and all the aches forgotten.

'Have I been long?' panted my mother. Then, as we made our way towards the gates, 'I've found a lovely coat for Mrs Todd, just what she wanted I think, and something for Mrs Bentley to wear at the wedding. There's just one more place but I thought you might be getting tired of waiting. When I've finished we'll go and have something to eat.'

We crossed the road and were soon making our way

along streets which were almost as narrow as the pavements. It was quiet here, hushed, as if a weight of noise had been lifted, and the soft shuffle-shuffle of footsteps and the clop of dray-horses' hoofs came intimate and distinct. We passed yawning cellar shafts where packages were being unloaded, and occasionally we passed a small restaurant, when there might come a whiff of frying fish.

It was quieter still when I followed our mother into the warehouse, so shabby and old that I felt quite disappointed. I had thought warehouses ('Wholesale and Shipping') would have been much more impressive.

'You stay here,' my mother whispered, 'the department is upstairs.'

I stood by the lift and watched her out of sight, and again set myself to wait. A door opened near me and a young woman with a pencil behind one ear emerged. She stopped and looked at us curiously.

'What a dear little baby. Does he belong to one of the staff?'

'No,' I managed to say, blushing. Looking rather puzzled, she walked briskly away.

Soon the office door opened again, and a man came out. He had left the door ajar, and inside I could see a sloping desk and a high stool with a seat covered in well-polished brown leather. The man looked at us over the top of his spectacles. Then he gestured with his thumb towards the office he had left. 'Go and have a sit down,' he said kindly, as he walked away.

Go and sit in there! I could hardly believe my ears. Could I perhaps have imagined it? Perhaps I *had* imagined it. I peeped at the stool; the brown, well-polished, padded leather seat shone with the rich colour of a date. I would no more have dreamed of going in and sitting on it than of resting upon a royal throne.

After a while the lift descended with our mother.

'Now I've quite finished. I've had a really good day today. We'll go to Stewart's for a treat, it's just near here. Then I must get something to take home.'

Together we entered the restaurant. 'We'll sit over there,' said our mother. 'I always come here when I've had an extra good day, the waitress knows me. Look, there she is.'

A buxom young woman came forward. She was like a country girl, with ruddy cheeks, double chin, and plentifully curling brown hair done in a bun at the back. She wore a starched white apron with a bib, and a cap with streamers, like an old-fashioned nanny in a picture.

'Isn't she nice,' our mother said. 'I expect they choose them like that specially.'

The waitress came towards us, smiling broadly.

'Is this yours?' looking at the baby.

'Yes, and this is my little girl. My other little girl is minding my shop.'

'*Well*,' said the waitress, 'you *must* be proud of them.' She took our order and put it on to a shelf in what looked like a cupboard, then pulled a cord and the shelves began to descend. Soon she hauled again, and up came our order complete with shining covers.

'Look over there,' whispered my mother when the waitress had left us, 'you see that woman? . . . A buyer! . . . *And* that one over there. I've seen them in the warehouses. They all seem to come here,' she said proudly.

'What's that stuff she's drinking?'

'Ssh! Stout.' Our mother's eyes held a faint suggestion of distaste and displeasure; the look with which she controlled the standards of our home.

*   *   *

Our shop opened at eight o'clock in the morning and stayed open until no more customers came in, usually about eight o'clock in the evening, except on Wednesdays, when it closed at one o'clock. Sometimes customers would be coming in all through meal-times, and on Saturday the bell might be ringing up to nine o'clock.

On Christmas Eve it would be after ten o'clock when the blinds were lowered, the last customers of all being husbands just out of the public houses who had forgotten to buy their wives presents: garrulous and unsteady, with nods and winks, they would buy for the most sedate of wives, lacy Celanese boudoir caps with rosebuds and satin ribbons; or fur garters, each garter having a little head with eyes, and a little tail.

Occasionally at meal-times when our mother had had no chance of eating, my sister would go into the shop when the bell rang, especially as it was usually the long-winded customers who came then and they would not be so inclined to stay chatting to a solemn twelve-year-old. And in the wake of the kind of customer who 'had the whole shop down' my sister would often go and stand beside our mother tidying the packets and boxes back into their right places.

I did little towards the shop apart from delivering parcels and taking orders to the post-box. My jobs were more in the house, and my main one was minding and taking out the baby.

Our mother would get him ready in the pram which stood in the living-room, and help me down the step into the passageway in front of the counter, and down a step again through the shop door on to the pavement. I was proud to be taking our baby out in the pram. Our mother stood at the door smiling, and saying, 'Goodbye, duckie. Mind how you go.' Innocently I smiled back, but our brother had many adventures while in my care.

I would often meet other girls out with their little brothers or sisters, and we would boast of our babies' achievements and progress. We would stop our prams, officiously tuck the covers in all round, and stroke the baby's hair back into its bonnet, as we had seen our mothers do. I could hardly wait for my brother to sit up. Usually, however, I was obliged to retreat to one of the quiet country lanes which led from the town, because my brother did cry so!

My first resort was the dummy, which our mother always put ready; if this failed, I dipped the dummy into

'my brother did cry so!'

the egg-cup containing honey which was kept in the corner of the pram; if this failed, I sang . . . then ran. Running would often have the desired effect. Whether it was that the bouncing surprised my brother and he fell asleep while thus distracted, or whether the motion soothed him to sleep, I did not know; when even running had no effect, I increased my pace, until in the end I was careering along as fast as I could run, the baby bumping helplessly up and down. Twice I tipped the pram right over, but fortunately our mother had taken the precaution of strapping the baby in, and I was able, after a struggle, to right the pram without him having suffered harm.

One of the roads I frequented had a small stream running beneath it at a certain point, the trickle of water being carried by a large pipe. Having put the brake on the pram, I descended one day to the stream to inspect it, and seeing the daylight showing at the far end of the pipe I felt impelled to crawl through. Thenceforward I gave myself this little treat each time I passed that way with the pram, the baby remaining unattended at the side of the road.

I was used to walking, and was at home out of doors, so our brother and I sometimes went for miles, coming home as the shop-windows were beginning to throw welcoming patches of light on to the pavements. Our mother would perhaps be standing behind the counter looking as if she had never stopped serving all the time we had been away. When I had negotiated the pram through the shop (the customers having obligingly squeezed up to make room for me) and was back in the living-room, I enjoyed lifting the baby out, warm as he was from his wrappings, his face fresh and rosy from the cold air.

He did not cry as much by the time summer came, and when the weather was warm I often took a book with me, and having come to a sufficiently quiet place, would sit on the side of the road for hours if he would allow, absent-mindedly jogging the pram—fiercely or gently as occasion demanded—to keep him satisfied or sleeping.

❖   ❖   ❖

There was no library in the town except for the one at the Institute which was for men, and the chemist's shelf of books—almost all love stories—from which our mother borrowed.

Reading was not then the reputable occupation it is now; not in our home at any rate, where it was regarded as a near-vice, not exactly comparable with opium-smoking but bearing dangerously in that direction. Even towards the end of her life, our mother never allowed herself to read a book before eight o'clock in the evening. Now, she never had time to do more than take a hurried look through the newspaper, except in bed at night. As for reading in bed, she would sometimes seem aghast at the thought of her own debaucheries—'Do you know, I read till half-past three last night!'

'Wretched reading!' my father would growl to no one in particular, as he heard a crash and noticed that either my sister or I was washing up with a book propped against the window-sill. We could do almost anything and read at the same time: knit and read, sew and read, peel potatoes and read. Books came to light under almost every cushion and behind almost every curtain. As well as books belonging to our parents and those we had received as presents over the years, which we read over and over again, my sister shared those our mother borrowed from the chemist's little library, and at first I shared them too.

In one of them the heroine had been trapped by the hero's ambitious mother (on her deathbed) into promising never to marry him. The book ended with the words '. . . and before her, lay the long weary years to come'. I could hardly bear the thought of it: all those long weary years dragging on and on! But I could see that, after all, she had promised.

However, I never did understand another anguished ending where, rather than spend the night alone with the heroine, the hero swam away to certain death from an island on which they had been marooned.

Whereas before the advent of the chemist's books my sister and I would sit pensively reading and rereading *A Basket of Flowers*, *The Wide Wide World*, *Worthy of his Name* ('Gentleman Gus'), *Melbourne House*, just sniffing occasionally or rubbing away a tear, we would now sit bolt upright, and our eyes, no longer screwed up to retain their moisture, would be wide open, as we followed the fortunes of the heroines of Ethel M. Dell, Elinor Glyn, and Ruby M. Ayres. Then, one terrible day, my sister went to our mother and told her very earnestly that the books from the chemist were not *fit* for me to read; so our mother, retreating shamefaced before the censure in my sister's firm brown eyes, forbade them to me.

On one occasion I had been tempted to disobey this edict, and my sister managed to wrest the forbidden book from my hand when I was at a very exciting part. I really did feel then that I could no longer go on living if I could not finish that book. It was called, I think, *Chandos Court*, and the heroine had just received a telegram: '. . . he was thrown from his camel and dragged . . .'. But my sister was intent upon doing her duty, and no amount of hair-pulling and biting could prevent her. Somehow I managed to get through the next day . . . and then the succeeding day . . . to take hold of life again, and carry on.

✻ ✻ ✻

About half-past five in the freshness of those summer mornings we were woken by our father and mother whispering and laughing under the window of our back bedroom. Our father had set up a rough bench in the yard, where he helped with the washing before he went to work.

Trade in the shop was good. Almost every day a whole page in the day-book was filled. There were regular customers now, whose measurements and idiosyncrasies our mother always remembered: whether they avoided green, or possessed a 46-inch hip, or wore Directoire knickers, or Lena Lastik vests, or thought of themselves as Small Women size when really they were WX. Now she had a young girl to take the baby out on weekdays, and someone to help in the house three mornings a week. There was a rail in the shop for coats and dresses, and the fixtures were becoming more and more stocked with packets and boxes. We had proper wrapping paper, and an advertisement in the church monthly.

Because space in our shop had been so limited, we now rented part of the chemist's shop-front, and the stock room behind it. It was that part of the premises the chemist's shop had taken over when it was expanding. The boundary had now moved back again, and our half a shop was once more a whole one.

In spite of all the progress, however, the struggle to pay the bills in time was almost as bad as ever, because of increased stock, a proportion of chronically bad payers, and the addition to our family. My sister was now eligible to take the scholarship, which sometimes one and perhaps two children from our school passed each year, proceeding then to the (otherwise fee-paying) local High School. Having passed the written work, however, she was visited on the day of the oral examination by a sick headache, and failed. There was a small family conference, and it was decided that she should go to a fee-paying secondary school in the next town.

13

ALL through the following winter I noticed, without asking why, that our mother was going out into the dark garden when the shop closed in the evening, and skipping. Not the smooth skipping of the girls at school, with their silky double turning of the rope ('What ho, she BUMPS! What ho, she BUMPS!'). Our mother's was hard, jolting, inexpert skipping, the rope flailing wildly at the ground, which went on and on until she seemed exhausted. But in August she gave birth to a little girl, and at the end of the term my elder sister left school to start work in our father's makeshift office.

Then, very suddenly, Mr John J. Marshall went broke, and my sister stayed at home helping in the shop and with the baby, while our father found work in the chair factory. Inexplicably, however, our father's chairs refused to stand up, and his fellows began to eye him with disfavour. He was a different kind of man from the craftsmen and near-craftsmen with whom he was working. Far from delighting in precision, he seemed to scorn if not actively to dislike it, and when, three months later, he saw an advertisement for temporary workers in the tax office, he left the factory and started work in the town nearby.

Meanwhile, a shop in the High Street was about to fall vacant, and it had been rumoured that a well-known drapery concern in the next town was considering it as a branch. It was a large shop with plate-glass windows and a high rent, but fearing competition our parents made a quick decision and took the shop themselves. Soon, with the help of the coalman's float, we moved with our worldly possessions the few hundred yards into the High Street, the chemist standing at her door to wave us goodbye.

Although our new shop was impressive, the building itself was very old, and had at one time been two cottages. Behind the shop premises, which were sunny and spacious, a long dark passage ran back past a staircase, a larder, and a sitting-room, to a small dark kitchen whose walls were distempered the colour of dried blood. In front of a disused fire-range, three small oil-stoves stood on a low form; there was also a pump, a stone sink, a copper, and a built-in dresser reaching almost to the ceiling and occupying most of the space of one wall. Two steps led up to a tiny scullery, which in turn led into an unlit, windowless, indoor bucket lavatory, open to the roof-space of the house and adjacent sheds—the sheds being full of rubbish and seemingly the dust of ages, as if they had been used over many years for a succession of purposes. Beyond there was a stable, a further bucket lavatory, a length of garden littered with scrap-iron, a cart-shed containing an old hay wagon, a pigsty, and some chicken-houses.

When living at the cottage we had become used to rats

and mice at threshing-time, and in the Square there had been a ceaseless struggle between the chemist and the rats from the farm on the other side of her shop; but all this was as nothing compared with the rats in our new home, where two doors away was a corn and hay merchant, and across the street another farm. Soon after we moved in, our mother met a rat coming downstairs as she went up, and as my sister and I lay in bed at night we could hear them scuttling about overhead, and would reach up crossly to bang on the sloping ceiling if they became too noisy.

Bit by bit the dirt was cleared away. In the kitchen the oil-stoves were discarded, the old range replaced by a modern fireplace, and the copper by a gas cooking-stove; the walls were redecorated, the dresser scrubbed and rescrubbed and its brass drawer-handles polished. In the sitting-room the green carpet was laid, and Lady Townsend, Herodias, and the monkey lawyers were hung on the walls.

'We always knock on the door before we go in,' our mother would say to visiting aunts when she showed them to the dark lavatory; she smiled her lovely warm reassuring smile, but I think the aunts had not the slightest idea of the significance of this little ceremony. Even I did not understand whether a rat might be expected to jump up out of the pail and bite me, or jump down on to my head from the loft above, but we had not been brought up to make a fuss, and I was able to keep my imagination in check. In any case the aunts came less and less. Our mother did not belong to them as she had done at the cottage, and with the babies we were all so busy.

Meanwhile, almost imperceptibly, the town was changing, and our mother's clientele began to include a different type of customer: customers with cars, customers whose husbands went to work in London each day, customers who confided troubles and problems of a different kind.

The town had been discovered, and now building was going on in the beautiful country surrounding it; quite big houses some of them, as well as a few houses put up by the Council.

The chair factory had moved to a site near the railway station: a few wooden huts including an office. Rumour had it that there had been success with a new method of spray polishing, and that there were plans for a sawmill, old horses being bought up for log-jugging, and timber being bought in the round.

At this point, to his surprise, our father was offered work in the office there, which he accepted.

14

A PARTY of fourteen-year-old girls from the Home was being prepared to emigrate to Canada. Now my two friends, Rose and Phyllis, invited me to their last communion before leaving the country. It was said of the Home girls that they went to every church service; now they were having a special one of their own. In the porch we said goodbye, and the girls, rosy-faced, scrubbed and shining, trotted off briskly into their new life two-by-two, the set of their boaters graduating from jaunty to demure.

I, also, was fourteen. My scholarship time had come and gone, the headmaster having told me that my parents did not want me to take the examination. It did not occur to me to ask them why, or even to mention the subject. Nor had it occurred to me to wonder what would happen to me when I left school, but when the day came my father told me that he had arranged for me to start work in the office at the chair factory.

In spite of early progress, the factory was now badly affected by the slump in trade, and our father, with his usual enthusiasm, had espoused its troubles as his own, identifying himself with its fate and with the fate of the increasing number of workers being stood off. There were so few orders. When he had realized just how few orders were coming in, he had been appalled. Impatient of inaction, he had at last asked to be allowed to leave the office and go in search of new customers. Much of the factory's trade had been with branches of leading furnishers in the North and in Wales, where now the slump was particularly bad. He would make use of his knowledge of London, the small shops as well as the large, to establish a better foothold there. Meanwhile, I should fill his place in the office.

I now earned fifteen shillings a week. Starting at eight-thirty in the morning, with an hour for lunch and half an hour for tea, I finished at six o'clock, working on Saturday mornings until one o'clock.

(*Fifteen shillings a week coming in regularly*. Sometimes I reverted still to my childish fears of being poor people in London, and with them returned the childish fantasy of our retreat, if it came to the worst, to a refuge in a grassy ditch. With fifteen shillings a week coming in regularly, that is if I did not get the sack, it would mean perhaps forty-two loaves: we should not starve. But it was so difficult to make the fantasy fit now. Even fantasy demands an element of reality to make it acceptable. Our mother, my sister, and me, in the ditch lined with dry grass, had been all very well; but now—all the extra people! Try as I would I could not get them to behave themselves. The children would keep popping up, and would not say, 'Not so very, very hungry, thank you, Mummy,' and as for our father . . .)

*   *   *

It was winter, and bleak at the factory. The makeshift offices were of wood with asbestos roofing, and were permeated by a strong smell of pear-drops and sawdust. They were joined to a long, low shed, the cushion shop, in which girls made up the flock-filled corduroy cushions for the chairs. Similar sheds, some larger, some smaller, were dotted about in all directions.

Both the cushion shop on one side and the Secretary's office on the other led into my office; there was also a door opening into the yard, on the further side of which was the packing shed. All day long packers would open the door from the yard, pass through my office, and open the door to the cushion shop, soon to emerge with arms piled high with cushions. The whirr of the sewing machines and the voices of the girls laughing and talking would come through the door as the forewoman held it open.

'That's right, Ernie, now you only need ten 534's and six 542's to make up that order.' She would close the door, and Ernie would stagger through my office and out into the yard, letting the outside door bang behind him.

Windows, and a sloping desk-top at which I sat on a high stool, ran the length of the wall opposite the yard door, and the half of my office nearest to the cushion shop was piled high with bales of cloth. Beneath the desk top were parcels of packing paper, and piles of small boxes, each box labelled, 'Domes of Silence'.

In my midway office, with my back to the life passing through, I felt isolated and odd. I knew that at different times, marked by a hooter, the men in the factory took their glue-pots off the round iron stoves and made themselves tea; and I knew the cushion girls also heated kettles and had refreshments. The Secretary, who lived nearby, disappeared at these times; but as such things had never been done at school, it did not occur to me to bring anything to the office to eat and drink.

There was another solitary person, a boy of my own age, taken on at the same time as myself. From the wages book I knew that he was paid ten shillings a week. All day, every day, he passed my window with a bucket, climbed the boundary fence, crossed the road, disappeared into the garden of a house there, emerged with the bucket now full of water, recrossed the road, reclimbed the fence, again passed across my window, and disappeared, continually to repeat his journey.

I was fortunate in that the Secretary, a partner in the firm, who now instructed me in the rudiments of office work, was a kind and scholarly man. He taught me well, and in accordance with his own meticulous standards. That I was so tongue-tied perhaps made him nervous, too, for his eyes seldom met mine, and his explanations were interspersed by dry little coughs.

'I see people sometimes (hmp hmp hmp) ... dirty people (hmp hmp hmp)' (he would look into an imaginary distance over the top of his spectacles) 'licking their fingers before turning the pages of ledgers—you may have seen something of the kind yourself—pages ruckled up and dirty at the top. I want you (hmp hmp hmp) to start from the beginning in the right way. Turn each page singly, like this ... *Never* lick the finger ...

'There are (hmp hmp hmp) people ... wicked men ... who will alter figures to change the value of cheques, so one must be very careful to rule lines right up to the figures, write very carefully without alteration, and add these words ...'

Together with the book-keeping, working out of wages, and other routine tasks, he taught me to keep the rubber stamps scrupulously clean—the letters well picked out with a pin—and how to press them firm and straight into the pad: no half-stamped or crooked imprints.

I typed the invoices, statements, and short letters, on the Underwood portable. First with two fingers, then spacing with my thumb, then—getting a little more accurate and speedy all the time—I imitated the lay-out of letters which came in from what I considered to be superior firms. Sometimes the Secretary would encourage me.

'Your typing is coming on already. If you improve your typing and perhaps (hmp hmp hmp) learn shorthand—Pitman's, I think I have a book somewhere—you will be a great help to me.' And with a long glance into that unseen distance—'Your handwriting is very good indeed. Makes it quite a pleasure to sign the cheques.'

Such praise was like manna from Heaven, yet I was still haunted by an idea that at any moment I might get the sack.

'You have a very bad head cold,' the Secretary said one day, 'have you ever thought of taking a nasal douche?'

Overwhelmed by the personal nature of the remark, I blushed, but said nothing.

'You get through a great deal of work; you don't get tired? No headaches, I hope?'

I blushed still more deeply. It did not occur to me to say that there was something amiss, which was that I was so COLD. His inner office with its one window and one door was kept from freezing point by the help of a round, single-burner Valor oil-stove, which he carried about the office with him. My office, with two of its three doors almost continuously open, had no heating whatsoever, and I had chilblains on my toes, and a broken chilblain on every finger of my left hand. My dripping nose and my dripping chilblains quite hindered me.

＊   ＊   ＊

On opening the ledgers I had found the familiar handwriting of my father. Usually spiky, like a demented temperature chart, it titled the pages here in beautiful copperplate, which I tried hard to emulate: 'S. Aston & Son, Ltd., Regent Street, Wrexham,' I wavered. 'Bladons, Ltd.,

Prospect Street, Hull. Lewis's, Ltd., Market Street, Manchester . . .'

On Fridays I worked out and paid the wages: time-cards collected and added up—42½ hours, 47 hours, 52½ hours, worked out at different rates; lists of piece-work brought in by the foremen, written on off-cuts of plywood and scraps of sandpaper; final deductions; the money spread out and counted into empty Domes of Silence boxes. Then the knife-edge—to balance the wages book, arrange the boxes of money in alphabetical order on shelves above a hatch in the Secretary's office wall, and be ready in time for the men—Adams, C., . . . Plested, R., . . . Spittles, G., . . . White, F. C., . . . Woodley, J. . . .

Soon the meaningless jumble of tasks, smells, noises, faces, and names began to make a pattern, crystallizing in the sight of the piles of chairs and chair-beds waiting in shrouds of straw and sacking for the railway company's truck; the 'adjustable hardwood chairs, Jacobean or fumed oak finish, with removable corduroy velvet flock-filled cushions, chairs sixteen shillings, or fourteen-and-sixpence in truckloads of fifty, chair-beds twenty-seven-and-sixpence, or twenty-six-and-sixpence in lots of six, terms five per cent prompt or two and a half per cent monthly account'. There they stood, their labels addressed in my own hand. They had been made from the piles of wood I saw lying about the yard 'in stick'; made and polished, cushioned and packed, by the workers whose faces appeared for a moment at the wages hatch on Fridays; who converged on the factory gates in the darkness of winter mornings in response to the early hooter; and who, on bicycles or on foot, made their way to the lighted sheds and the little world of glue-pots, work benches, revolving tables, and football sweeps.

The Domes of Silence beneath my desk were nothing more romantic than castors, and the bales of cloth in the corner were of 'corduroy velvet', covering for the 'removable flock-filled cushions'—the flock, in its turn, being that something which I ordered forty sacks at a time from somewhere called Hebden Bridge. The polish being sprayed on to those revolving chairs which I glimpsed when passing the polishing shed, was that for which *I* wrote orders, and cheques in payment.

Meanwhile, to be first on the buyers' doorsteps, our father caught the early workmen's train. Our mother, seeing him off in the freshness and early light, across the yard and to the side door, would pick him a flower for his buttonhole from the border he had planted, and stand back to admire him—his bowler hat, his rolled umbrella, and the attaché case which now, instead of nappies, held the photographs of chairs and samples of corduroy. In the evenings, when the shop was closed and she sat at the table mending, he told her of his day, his eager voice rising, his eyes bright with indignation.

'There we all are, just waiting. Over two hours, waiting. Just *sitting there*. Then the buyer comes. Puts his head round the door. "You can all go, the whole lot of you. Yes, off you go! No, I won't see anyone. No, nothing doing."

'They don't so much as let me get my photographs out. "Never heard of you!" they say, but I *know* they can really sell our chairs there. You'll see, those chairs are going to sell like hot cakes!'

A day came when he reported an order for one chair—'just to get me out of the way; fed up with me hanging round them'. Then slowly and painfully his connection increased, the trickle of orders passing through the order book sustaining for the moment the dwindling volume of orders in hand.

One day a friendly buyer in the Old Kent Road took him to a cheap lodging-house. 'You're always wondering what kind of people sleep on your old chair-beds. Come with me and I'll show you something.'

It was a tall house, and the way was up flights of stairs. The door was opened by a man in his shirt-sleeves, and then our father saw that apart from four familiar chair-beds, the room was devoid of furnishings.

The chair-beds were placed one in each corner of the room. Our father told us how he had crossed over and pressed his knuckles into one of the flock cushions. As he had expected, it had become thin, hard, and lumpy with use.

'Poor devils! I reckon they could do with a few springs.'

15

ONCE again our mother was expecting a baby, and this time there was unspoken dismay. After the birth of our sister, Grandma Davies had turned to our mother as she was saying goodbye. 'Remember,' she had said, 'no more babies. If there is another, remember, I shan't come.'

True to her word, when our new brother was born she did not come. At first all went well enough, but on the third day everything began to go wrong. The doctor came several times, the district nurse was in the house for most of the day, our father and I both stayed away from work, and then another nurse made her appearance. The next day it was decided that our mother should go into hospital.

While the children were having their tea that day I went to say goodbye to our mother. She seemed to be asleep. Her face was a curious greenish colour and was bathed in perspiration. Every now and then she gave a violent shudder.

The nurse had been doing her hair. She had parted it in the middle and had brushed it down flat and straight each side, plaiting it into hard, tight little plaits. I looked at the nurse.

'She wouldn't want her hair to be like that; she likes it to be puffed out.'

'I think it will do for now,' said the nurse. She spoke kindly but with a certain firmness. Then I saw something worse.

'She wouldn't want to be without her teeth; she would hate anyone to see her without her teeth, she keeps them in even at night.'

'I don't think she will be needing her teeth.'

'She will be wanting to wear her gold wrist-watch if she is going away.' It was not really her watch, it was mine. Aunt Kate had sent both my sister and me 'gold' watches, but mine was too good for me to wear yet. I lent it to my mother sometimes, but now, for some reason, it pleased me to call it hers.

'I don't think she will be needing a watch,' said the nurse. She was packing a case, and went to get more things.

The case lay open on the floor. I looked round the room. On the mantelpiece I saw a glass, and in the glass our mother's teeth. Quickly I took a handkerchief from the box on the dressing-table, lifted the teeth dripping from the glass, and wrapped them in the handkerchief. Then I pushed them well down into the corner of the case. The watch would be in the top drawer; I found it, and put it under the nightdresses.

To keep the children out of the way while the ambulance came, I put them into the pram and took them for a walk along the straight road lined with telegraph poles which led out of the town. Muriel Simpkins, on holiday as usual, must have seen me, because soon I heard her bicycle bell and she drew up and cycled slowly beside the pram.

We continued for a while in silence, then she said, 'Do you think your father will marry again if your mother dies?

My mother says he will have to with five children on his hands.'

I stopped the pram. 'Dies! She's not going to *die*.'

'My mother says people don't get over what your mother's got. Mrs Watkins told my mother that your father was very rude to Dr Samuels, and won't believe anything he says, and now he's asked for a specialist to be sent down from London to see her in hospital. A specialist from London! Just think what that will cost. And all a waste of money my mother says.' Slowly and expertly she circled in the road; then, bracing her back, she shot off back to the town.

It was beginning to get dark, and I too turned and made my way back. As I passed along the pavement in the light

'*I heard her bicycle bell*'

of the shop-windows, Mrs Wilkins came right out of her shop and called after me. It was the first time I had ever seen her out of doors.

'I thought I saw you,' she panted, 'how's your mother then? How is she?'

'Not very well, she's gone to hospital.'

'I'm very sorry to hear it. It's bad, very bad.' She shook her head. 'Tell her I was asking after her if you have a chance, will you?' She turned, and climbed ponderously up the steps into her little shop.

At home there was the dreadful empty feeling of a house from which the mother has gone. My sister was tidying the shop, and after putting the children to bed I wandered aimlessly into the kitchen. Our father had returned from the hospital and was sitting at the table, on which, although it was not Saturday, was a pile of bills. I stood beside him, and saw he was making a list—our debts. As I watched, the column lengthened and lengthened. At last I could bear it no longer. 'Is it very bad?'

My voice sounded cracked and breathless in the quiet kitchen. I didn't even know why I asked, because of course I knew the answer: we shall go broke, we shall all end in the workhouse. But to my surprise, our father turned in his chair and looked at me. Then he smiled, kind and reassuring, almost like our mother. 'Nothing for you to worry about, my dear,' he said cheerfully. And perfectly satisfied I went into the shop to help my sister.

Because ours was a house of sadness and sickness customers kept tactfully away. Now our father put his head round the door. 'I should close,' he said. 'No one will come in tonight.'

We had been living for the last few days almost as if besieged, forgetting the world outside, and caring nothing for what was going on in the town, so we did not know that our mother had been prayed for in church, a sure sign that a person is expected to die. We did not guess the pitch of concern about our affairs, and when we lowered the shop-blinds two hours earlier than usual we did not realize the conclusion the customers would draw. We did not know there were those who had heard of, and had come to see the lowered blinds, nor did we see their tears.

'Poor woman! Poor woman! And all those motherless children.'

16

WE emerged from this difficult time feeling rather as a butterfly might, when fresh from its chrysalis it rests for a moment on a leaf, delicate and rather wobbly, yet sensing as never before (because of its new, thin skin) the tenderness of the sunshine and the subtle fragrances of the summer breeze, before hardening to the struggle for existence. We were in that brief period after trouble when those around close in to comfort until one is (or should be) on one's feet again, and fit to face life as it is.

Customers offered to massage our mother's head, temporarily bald from the fever, on which she now wore a black silk cap. Others crocheted or knitted thicker caps, some strangely shaped, against the cold weather. Chickens and jellies found their way into our larder. Bad payers paid, and everywhere people smiled at us and said how glad they were to see our mother back. Although I had been away from work for almost three months, my job had been kept open for me, and I was to start again in a fortnight's time.

In the evenings, when the children were in bed, we went into the sitting-room and our mother played some songs, which we all sang——strange, inappropriate songs they seemed to me, from a book our father had dug up from somewhere:

> Jolly young Jacks are we;
> Merry of heart and gay;
> Sons of the rolling sea . . .

There seemed to me to be something light-headed about our parents' singing.

The sleeping arrangements had been changed round again to make place for the new baby, and now I slept in one of the stock-rooms on a dais caused by the raising of the height of the shop ceiling to accommodate the plate-glass windows. Around me were fixtures which had been there before we came and which now held our stock. I was sleeping on one of our father's abortive folding beds; sometimes the end third would collapse in the night, letting my legs and the bed-clothes down with it, and sometimes the top third would collapse, letting down my head and the pillow, but in the relief of our mother's recovery such nocturnal adventures were as nothing.

My nightly companion now was a 'corset lady'. Not the modest pink satin 'Twilfit' corset lady, of which our elder brother was so fond, and which he would often pause wonderingly to caress as he trotted through the shop, but one which had been banished because of complaints from a customer that it was 'suggestive'. The model was very striking and perhaps a little before its time. It had solid green Medusa-like locks, and a smooth bronze body.

Now on my way to bed I passed through the dark shop; and through the glass of the shop door, I could see across the street the fanlight of the house opposite—an oblong of warm yellow light. The maiden ladies who lived there had given us a present of a jar of boiled sweets for Christmas, and the light seemed to say, 'Friends live here, all is well.'

After I had climbed the wooden, ladder-like steps to my stock-room, I went first to look through the window of the back stock-room, to where I could see below another yellow light—a small square kitchen window high in the brick wall of the house next door and overlooking our back yard. Through that window an arm would sometimes come, and a voice gasp, 'For your mother, dear; a little cold chicken with my love, tell her.' And again the yellow light seemed to say, 'All is well, a friend lives here.'

My bed was to one side of the front window, while the corset lady was on the other side. Light from an occasional passing car would shine through the uncurtained window, momentarily to play over the handsome bronze features of my companion; and even this light seemed to bear comfort, to say, 'All is well now, all is well.'

✻   ✻   ✻

The trade we had lost returned, but could not now stem the tide of bills swollen by hospital, doctors' and specialists' fees, and the extra expenses of a long illness. Already many of the warehouses were threatening proceedings, and times were too bad and our situation held too much risk for the bank to consider an overdraft. Bankruptcy seemed inevitable, although strangely it did not seem to matter any more.

A new phrase came into our parents' conversation—'a meeting of creditors'—and they no longer confined their business talks to when they were alone together; in the evenings their conversation was unceasingly of bills and bankruptcy and the threatened meeting of creditors. The plight of the factory was forgotten. In matters of business our mother, true Victorian that she was, tended to accept our father's judgements, but now, at this eleventh hour, she rebelled.

'Why won't they wait a little longer! Just because we've had some bad luck it shouldn't mean the end of a good business that was growing. I shall go and tell them so, and ask them to wait just a little longer.'

'I've been through all that with them over and over again,' our father's voice was flat and tired. 'And after all, they can't be expected to support all these little businesses, they've got their own troubles.'

'I shall go, anyway. And after that, we'll have a really big sale, to raise every penny we can. And then, there's your idea for a cheap chair-bed with springs—your "Superest"! You'd forgotten all about that, hadn't you. You're always such an old Gummidge. Haven't you got five lovely children, and every one perfect! I shall go to all the firms we owe money to and ask to see the director and refuse to go until I have seen him, and I shall tell him they might be very glad to have our account one day.'

She dressed very carefully when the day for her venture came, and in her bag was a list of all our creditors. We could not expect her back before six o'clock, but still she had not come when our father returned from work, so without waiting for tea he went straight to the station to meet her.

When later they came home together, our spirits rose; we could tell just by the look of them that the news was good. Our mother, almost voiceless with talking, was jubilant. The majority of our creditors had agreed to wait. Bankruptcy, for the time being, had been warded off.

17

So far, so good. And now began the preparations for our great sale.

We had never had a sale before: our mother had always prided herself that everything in her shop was clean stock, and saleable—any exceptions we used ourselves or put in the bargains basket on the counter. Now that we must have a sale our parents agreed that no ordinary one would suffice. It must be a real sale: every bit of stock not needed for the coming season must be turned out and prices reduced to a level at which everything was sure to sell.

The day was fixed for a Saturday, when our father could be there to take money to the bank, and I could have half a day off from work and help to serve. The shop-windows were dressed with sales goods and the blinds remained up every night during that week.

We were awakened on the morning of the sale by a curious and rather frightening noise, a noise quite new to us. It was a dry shuffling noise on the pavement below our windows. Cautiously peeping out, we found to our horror that a large crowd of people was jostling outside—a crowd which extended well down the High Street. With awe we realized that it was because of *our shop* that this throng of people had risen and breakfasted early and left their housework to gather on our pavement by seven o'clock in the morning. They had come, summoned by the messages we had printed with crayons and paints: 'Less than half-price!' 'All in this pile 6*d*.' 'In all sizes 2*s*. 6*d*.' They had been lured there by the bronze corset lady who, for a day, had been brought from retirement. Suggestive or not suggestive, she now stood in the window well to the fore, seducing passers-by in a scarlet woollen dress reduced to 2*s*. 6*d*.

We retreated from our bedrooms overcome by stagefright, and although the shop door was locked, we breakfasted furtively, speaking only in whispers, as if the house were surrounded by a pack of wolves.

Just before eight o'clock, pale and self-conscious, our mother, my sister and I took our places behind the counter, each with a pad and pencil and a pair of scissors suspended from a string round the waist. Our brother had been promised the honour of unlocking the shop door, but he almost lost his nerve when he saw through the shop-window the seething mass of customers; talking and laughing good-naturedly enough, yet each with a businesslike glint in her eye, and a determination not to lose her place. However, as the Market Square clock struck eight, he plucked up his courage and darted forward, turned the key in the lock, then ran for dear life as the customers surged in.

The foremost made a dive for the window. Knocking

over stands, piles of stockings, and everything in her path, she seized the bronze corset lady triumphantly in her arms. Others ran frantically from pile to pile until their arms were full, when flushed and loquacious they came to have their bargains listed. Fat ladies squeezed themselves into tight dresses and thin ladies draped themselves in loose ones, posing before the mirror trying to persuade themselves that they fitted.

'Look! Lil, Lil, come over here. This looks all right, doesn't it? Not too tight? Or do you think it would be better for Gladys... or Vera? It's such a bargain.' Regretfully they would throw one thing down and pick up another. 'Lil, Lil, come over here. What do you think of

'plucked up his courage'

this, then?... Yes, perhaps it is a bit on the short side, what a pity.'

A tiny boy stood in a corner where his mother had placed him for safety. He clasped in his arms a pair of corsets nearly as big as himself. Wide-eyed he watched the women rushing here and there picking things up, flinging them down, and sorting feverishly through piles of

'he watched the women'

stockings or vests to find their sizes. Some keen-eyed customers carried over their arms stockings by the dozen, buying for daughters, neighbours, and friends. Some seemed to have bought enough vests to last them for the rest of their lives.

Dazed, but struggling to keep efficient, we added up columns of figures, took sheaves of banknotes from trembling hands, ran to the overflowing till, gave change, tied up mountains of parcels, gave our judgement on fittings, and vainly tried to keep the customers and the sales goods in some sort of order.

By ten o'clock the rush was over. The shop looked as if a tornado had passed by, the windows denuded except for an odd sock or two, and the bronze corset lady leaning drunkenly against the rail. The counter was a sea of stockings, vests, knickers, and blouses, which customers had taken up and thrown down, attracted by something better.

By the afternoon trade was quite leisured. Latecomers picked about happily in the remains, which had been tidied and regrouped. Soon after ten o'clock that night we let down the blinds and locked the door. Everything was gone.

To what extent the day's takings might encourage our creditors, we had little idea. But the sight of all those customers! All that money! Tired out though we were, and in spite of ourselves, a feeling began to grow that we might yet escape the trouble hanging over us.

18

THE next year, that grey anxious year, was the year in which we had mumps and measles.

Our father was having a bout of duodenal ulcer trouble, living first on milk which he disliked, then on cod which he said reminded him of dead bodies, and then on chicken which we could ill afford. Haunted by the spectre of bankruptcy and visions of cheap chair-beds with springs, he was preoccupied and edgy, and surrounded by that disturbance of the air common with inventors. It weighed upon our convalescent spirits, but by now we all realized as well as he did that the position at the factory was desperate, and that the length of time they could keep going in the hope that trade would revive had almost run out.

One evening while our mother was emptying the till and counting the precious banknotes, our father came and asked her for money so that he could hire a car and driver and take his Superest to London; the firm, he said bitterly, had not enough faith in him to back it to that extent. He had at last contrived a spring base whose simplicity made possible production at the low cost necessary, and a sample chair-bed had been assembled. Dejected, hardly caring, he set off for London, and as we watched the car drive away and turn the corner at the top of the High Street, we shook our heads over our father and his old Superest.

So infected by his mood of gloom were we, so confirmed in our attitude of tolerant scepticism to everything he did, that when he returned with a tale of triumph it was we who were hard to convince. Those old pieces of wire our father had tinkered with and puzzled over, could they really be of any importance? Could such an inexpert homely thing as our father's Superest really make any difference to the factory's troubles, to that crowd of workers making their way through the gates on dark cold mornings? Could people in London really take it seriously—go into shops and *buy* it?

And astonishingly the answer came: in tales of orders 'pouring in', of orders being repeated and increased, later to continue in a steady confident rhythm, while the factory weathered the storm and the crisis became a thing of the past; a prelude to greater things.

19

THERE came a time when I began to notice a change in our parents' ways.

'Just run and get a half of best butter.'

Or our father would bring home something which seemed to me quite unnecessary: an old gramophone with a horn and some records; a cut-glass bowl with a tarnished silver rim.

Quite often now we had a chicken for dinner on Sundays. Our mother, by nature wholesale in housekeeping as in buying for the shop, loved taking in the large number of loaves our family needed, bountifully cracking the eggs into the frying-pan at breakfast-time, and giving her large order to the grocer. Every time a delivery boy or a parcel man brought something to the shop or subscriptions were called for, her hand went happily to the till. At Christmas-time my sister and I delivered quite a number of parcels, 'little somethings' for people who had helped her in some way during the year. And occasionally, now, she would buy 'a special' for herself, 'because of the shop'.

Sometimes my sister or I would accompany our father or mother to London when they went, for a treat. But the London each showed us was very different. When I went with our mother, everything seemed clothed in romance. How the buses bounded along! London was all green trees and parks, sunshine and floating white clouds, marble arches, mounted police, Big Ben, Nelson, the river, and 'on the steps of St Paul's', where we might have arranged to meet aunts. It seemed almost as if London was a connection of ours; everything was famous and familiar, and in some way part of us.

One day we called on Aunt Winifred. We found her sitting behind her desk, full of authority. 'I saw the others the last time I came up,' my mother was saying. 'We did enjoy ourselves . . .'

Aunt Winifred heard her out in silence. Only when my mother had finished did she raise her eyes. 'Amy, tell me,' she said quietly. 'Who paid?'

My mother considered her gloved hands, and smiled. 'I did,' she said at last.

When I went with our father, I saw the seamy side. It was usually necessary for us to go south of the river to attend to the business he had to do. He seemed to know the way everywhere: through streets and alleys and back yards in districts perilously near to being poorer parts, where one day we ended up in a kind of loft and I was left waiting while my father had a long talk with a man who wore a bibbed apron and carried a glue pot.

'Quite a clever chap, that. I suppose we ought to be getting something to eat. There's a place over there where they sell quite good little pies. They're a ha'penny cheaper than most of them round here.'

We entered a bleak little shop with bentwood chairs and tea-ringed tables, steamy windows and a wet floor, and my father ordered two pies and two cups of tea—'A good strong one for me, please.'

'You always say you can't eat pork,' I said.

'Pork?'

'Yes, pork. You always say that pork is poison to you. And that tea you've got—it's enough to kill anybody. No wonder you get indigestion.'

Afterwards we made our way back through the more dreary parts, he pausing every now and then to look into some grimy window. I could see he relished every cobweb.

'That's a very nice jug, isn't it? I've never seen one quite like that before. That gilt . . . I think I'll just go and have a better look. Perhaps your mother would like it.'

'What does she want a jug for? It's you who want it, and it's just being extravagant.'

Directly he was back outside the shop he unwrapped his prize. He couldn't take his eyes off it.

'Only a pound. Your mother will love this.'

Only a pound! He was as bad as our mother. They were both awful, and they were both *extravagant.*

(But seventeen-and-six a week coming in regularly . . . about fifty loaves. That should be enough if it came to the worst. And perhaps there was no real need to worry about getting the sack. Even if I did get the sack I could perhaps get another job; things were rather better now. And my sister was starting work—our mother was to have a proper assistant in the shop. Perhaps there was no need to worry any more?)

'Did you have a good time?' my mother, all beams and smiles, greeted us. 'What did you have for dinner?'

'A horrible little pork pie, and a cup of tea,' I said.

'Oh *Hendry*, I told you.' All the same she couldn't help laughing, she knew him so well. She called him Hendry, and he called her Husk, or Husket, or Husky Dream, because she had always been so chesty.

᠅   ᠅   ᠅

And then our father really did break out. He bought a car.

It was an enormous tourer and cost five pounds. Once it must have had immense dignity and power. Its dignity was lost; the hood was missing altogether, and the once imposing headlamps were battered and broken and quite unusable. But its power? That was an unknown quantity; our father was completely innocent of knowledge of cars.

It was so big that it only just managed to get through our garden gates. The man who brought it backed it carefully in and went away, and we all stood round gazing at it. Our car.

'None of us can drive,' said my sister at last.

'George Watson has just taught me; it's easy enough really,' said our father, 'and now that we have a car we shall be able to go to the sea.' He had a passion for the sea.

It was decided that we should waste no time but go to the sea the next Sunday, and on the Saturday, Grandma Davies—recently widowed and staying with us for a while—my sister and I, cut sandwiches and packed biscuit tins bought from the grocer with enough food to last eight people for a day. That evening we loaded the car, adding a kettle, some dry wood, and our mackintoshes. The sky was very red when the sun went down, and I prayed that the next day would be dry and that we should be brought safe home before lighting-up time.

Soon after six o'clock, on a pearl-grey morning, in a mist which promised sunshine, we climbed into the car. Our father cranked it up and took his place, and we were off. The town, as we drove out, was quiet as a town in a dream; we met no one and saw no living thing, not even a dog.

My sister sat next to our father; she had been given a list of the towns we should pass through, and her job was to watch the signposts. My job was to crank the car if it stalled.

Soon the town was left behind, and we were making our way between misty fields, and hedges dripping with moisture. 'Isn't the air lovely,' murmured Grandma as we bowled along, 'so fresh.' It was indeed fresh, if not downright cold, as, unprotected as we were, it whistled round our ears, tugged at our hair, and sent Grandma's long, black crêpe widow's weeds streaming out behind her. With her pale cameo profile she looked like a rakish Queen Victoria perched there in the back seat, dignified among the tins, mackintoshes, and children.

Our father, grim and edgy, looked fixedly ahead; beside him my sister, serious and concentrating hard, called instructions. 'Left at this fork,' she shouted. 'No, no, no—oh, I'm so sorry, no, it's the other road.'

Our father stopped the car and turned to her. 'Well, which is it? Make up your mind.'

'It's the other way; you'll have to back.' But the car had stalled.

Jumping out with the handle, I cranked; there was no response. Again I turned the stiff heavy handle—again and again and again, while anxious faces peered down at me from the car. At last there came a roar.

'Come on, come on, get in before it stops again,' shouted our father, and then, after much experimenting, we proceeded backwards in great sickly lurches.

Fortunately our mother, not being of an anxious disposition, was looking about her enjoying to the full the air, the beautiful countryside, and the novelty of our erratic course. She had one fear only, that we should roll down a steep hill backwards.

Soon, passing village churches, we heard their private muted morning bell, and met people on their way to early service looking, with their hats, gloves, and sometimes prayer-books, so tidy, so good, so *safe*—as recklessly we rattled onwards to the sea.

Then the sun broke through the mist and we came to the wonderful glittering river, the white paint of the riverside houses sparkling with dew. We saw the waiting craft, and the rich gardens whose lawns were such a velvety deep

green, the flowers so scarlet, white, or blue in the morning
sun. All seemed to be sleeping as we passed, only we and
the churchgoers seemed to be awake.

We were on the outskirts of a small town when the
puncture came. We all felt it, and our father, my sister, and
I jumped down. The tyre was quite flat. Our father gazed
at it helplessly and there was a tactful silence.

But someone was watching us: Sir Galahad, in the shape
of a short, fat man, who opened his garden gate, and
approached. 'Saw you through the window. I like that, I
thought, not leaving it all to their dad. Now I've got a car
myself, and perhaps I can be of service.'

When the time came to say goodbye, Sir Galahad patted
our father's arm. 'Not at all, not at all. A very interesting
car you've got there.'

More cars were on the road now and the sun, climbing
up the sky, was rather too bright and a little too warm.
Now, at a junction, we might have to wait, when the
engine would often stall. Scarlet with embarrassment and
heat, my shoes sticking in the melting tar of the road, I
would turn the handle again and again, while gradually a
queue of impatient travellers with waving arms and angry
voices formed behind us.

Passing through a village we saw a wheel bounding along
the road in front of us. 'Look!' the children cried
wonderingly, pointing, 'a *wheel!*'

Then our car sank sideways and we began to bump.

It was my sister who kept her head. She pointed to the
boys who were beginning to gather. 'Offer a shilling to the
one who brings the wheel back,' she advised our father,
'and another shilling to the one who brings a garage man!'

How familiar every tree became, every garden, and every
shop-window in that village street, as we walked the
children up and down waiting for the car to be mended—
every stick and stone an old acquaintance—and when at

last we were again on our way, another hour nearer to lighting-up time, and with another hour for the weather to have a chance of changing, we had become quiet and subdued. Days and weeks seemed to have passed since we set out on our journey. It seemed impossible that it was still the morning, and that we might still reach the sea and be home again before lighting-up time.

Then, ahead, we saw the downs, swelling away into the distance. Beyond those downs, so implacably steep, lay the sea.

Our time of trial came when, some miles later, we turned a corner to be confronted by the sight I had been dreading—a long, steep hill. With a jerk, our father changed into bottom gear, and slowly we began to grind our way up. Almost at the top the gradient increased. It was too much; the car laboured a little further, then stopped moving.

'We're going backwards!' screamed our mother. '*We're going backwards!*'

We tried to soothe her although the car did seem to be slipping a little.

'There's no need for a lot of sensation,' said our father agitatedly, 'just get out, some of you bigger ones, and give a push.'

With alacrity we all started jumping down, all except Grandma, who was hemmed in by biscuit tins, and the youngest who was sleeping soundly on the capacious floor of the back row.

'No, not you,' said our father testily, as Grandma began to extricate herself, 'but lean forward, lean forward.'

He turned to the controls, and I cranked and cranked. Soon the engine was going again and then, as we all pushed, the car began to move. Painfully, sometimes inch by inch, sometimes in short runs, slipping, stumbling, with pauses for rests and fits of giggles, we reached the top.

And now there was a new emptiness in the air, and a faint, long-remembered smell. We were approaching the sea.

*   *   *

The children were singing as we made our way home. Our father, too, was more confident; the car was steadier and more amenable, well in its stride and seeming to move forward willingly, like an old horse making for its stable.

Back we went past the little churches, where now the congregations were coming from evensong; past the village greens with cricket matches in progress; past the river, thronged with craft and romantic with shadows and laughter and snatches of music; past the water meadows and Marlow Bridge.

Then we were getting on to our home ground. The houses of the town were wrapped in Sunday quiet, and suddenly conscious of our flaming faces and dishevelled hair, we were glad to turn into the lane which ran behind the High Street. It was more private there, and there at last were our gates open to receive us. Home!

But to our surprise our father did not turn in; ignoring the welcoming gates he continued to drive along the lane.

We looked at him in amazement. He seemed embarrassed. 'I'll just take her round again,' he muttered apologetically, a little red in the face. 'Rather a tight fit; couldn't have cleared it at that angle.'

We settled back in our places.

The lane continued circling, then led into the Square. Here a preacher, his wife and two young daughters were holding a service by themselves as they did most Sunday evenings in summer—'My friends . . .' the preacher would say, raising an admonitory hand to the empty Square. When dressed in our Sunday clothes, with the knowledge that we had been to Sunday school and church twice already that day, and that even now our mother was

playing hymns, we had felt a little irritated that he should
yet have the power to make us feel wicked.

But now it was different. Dishevelled, windswept,
obvious Sabbath-breakers, well may he look at us with
disapproval, and we bent our heads.

Driving self-consciously up the almost deserted High
Street, under the gaze of curtained upper windows, we met
Mr Todd the bank manager with his wife and their three
children, evidently taking a walk after chapel. We blushed.
Their impeccable tidiness, rightness, and virtue made us
feel more bedraggled than ever, but courteously Mr Todd
raised his hat, and Mrs Todd smiled—although a little
stiffly. Our mother acknowledged their greeting with a
smile, and Grandma, from her lofty seat, gave a gracious
inclination of the head.

Then we were back in the lane and approaching our
gateway. '*Now*,' we shouted, 'turn. It's easy, *turn!*' But
again our father shot past.

'Sorry, sorry,' he muttered, 'next time.'

Continuing still along the lane, we encountered a gang of
boys playing on bicycles. They paused to stare. 'Look at
that old wreck!' Derisive whistles pursued us out of sight.

Now the Square, and there again was the preacher. His
arm was raised ('My friends . . .'). He seemed almost to be
greeting us. There was no need, I thought resentfully, to
try and make us feel wicked, we felt wicked already. But
the peering, short-sighted eyes held no reproof, only a mild
astonishment.

Then once more we were in the High Street. Perhaps at
least the Todds would have gone by now but no, they were
almost upon us, and this time it was more than surprise—
almost alarm—that showed in Mr Todd's eyes. Even our
mother blushed a little.

'They think we're dotty,' said my sister, painfully.

'Or swanking.'

134

We relieved our feelings in helpless giggles. Now, as we approached the gates, a look of grim determination was on our father's face.

*   *   *

The car cleared the gateposts with half an inch to spare and came to rest.

For a time we sat speechless, limp with relief, half stupefied, now movement had ceased, by the effects of long exposure to sun and wind. We had been to the sea and we had come home again. It had not rained and the sun had not set.

Oh, home! How peaceful, how desirable it looked. The sun's last rays, slanting over the tiled roofs of the High Street shone full in our faces. The children, hair bleached and faces ruddy, were like so many birds in a nest. Between its high brick walls the garden was beautiful in the flattering light of evening: no longer a derelict part of the town, graveyard of drowned kittens, old bedsteads, and rubbish, it was a cottage garden. With incorrigible artistry our father had embedded pieces of broken blue plates to make a mosaic of the little concrete path, and had screened behind a battalion of sunflowers the old pigsty and hen-houses. Shadows concealed the shed where next season's stock, just in, was waiting to be unpacked and priced, and the smaller shed housing our father's latest brainwave. But the little lawn gleamed emerald, and the pure colours of the flowers—geums, cornflowers, and marigolds—shone intense, gem-like, in the rich golden rays of the sun.

At last our father moved, and descended stiffly from his seat. We sat on, while he surveyed us in our car.

For the first time I realized that he was really quite handsome. His eyes were mocking and very bright.

'The Rich Mrs Robinson!' he said.

From her perch among the biscuit tins and children she looked down at him, and smiled.

Some day, I shall be rich.

Epilogue

'Is that all it's going to be!'

OUR father had always tended to like things upside-down and back-to-front, to have affinity with the poet who preferred things 'counter, original, spare, strange', while our mother had always liked things to be just so, and not, as she would grumble to our father, 'all piggy'.

In the past a balance had been kept, but now our father was tending to get the bit between his teeth—bringing milk to the table in a gravy-boat saying he didn't see how it should change the taste of the tea, and boldly wearing his pullover with the V at the back trying to pretend he couldn't tell the difference.

But his wife fought on.

'Before you do anything else,' she would say desperately when I came in the morning, 'would you just move that mat; it *is* crooked, isn't it. I don't like to say anything to Daddy because he's so good, but he does it every day. I think sometimes he puts it like that on purpose, because he *likes* things crooked. I could hardly wait till you came.'

His job had come to an end during the war and he had spent most of his time and ingenuity on voluntary work—scheming schemes for raising money for comforts ('Our Own Forces Fund') and manoeuvring with the Home Guard. Our mother, who might have been expected to be making a small fortune, did not fare much better from a financial point of view; there were so many parcels to be sent, bombed-out relations to be helped, evacuees, good causes, appeals, sad stories and prices marked down. And the war had taken it out of people: like so many others, they too had lost a son.

With the one incurably unbusinesslike, and the other incurably generous, they later retired, having saved what they hoped might be enough money to live on but with no claim to old-age pensions. They retired to the cottage in which our father had been born and which his sister now let to him at a favourable rent.

✻   ✻   ✻

The cottage stood among the new dwellings in the village like a very old lady. There was the same desiccated complexion and aura of mortality.

There were attics in the cottage, and a cellar, and it was quite a long walk from the downstairs room our mother had at last consented to use as their bedroom to the kitchen and bathroom.

The doors had brass doorknobs, even the doors to the little cupboards by the chimney-piece. The windows were leaded and could be lifted right off their brackets to be cleaned.

Here they had been able to exercise their complementary flairs for home-making to the full: the pictures, the old ornaments, the interesting chairs which had been bought over the years all revealed their beauty and hid their flaws and cracks in the dim cool light of the old cottage; the curtains, the loose covers, and the little touches, were exactly what was needed. (It would have looked different in days gone by, when there had been always twenty pairs of boots in the house, and when the bare wooden floors of all the bedrooms had been scrubbed through once a fortnight. Or in the days when there had been roast pork for breakfast, and beer.)

Increasing deafness had forced our mother to give up the

shop she had come to love. This, and now an unsuccessful hip operation, left her suddenly, and without warning, *a cripple!* After that first moment of disbelief and bewilderment, however, she returned to the subject no more.

If the doorbell rang, our father would answer it, appearing perhaps in an apron (for had he not been

'like a very old lady'

enjoying his daily miracle of washing up the breakfast things in a teacupful of water?), and in some clever way becoming, on his journey to the front door, a poor old man, shoulders a little bent, shuffling a little, his wiping-up cloth hanging ostentatiously over one arm.

'How is Mrs Robinson?'

'Not very well, I'm afraid, not well enough to see anyone. If you'll excuse me . . .' (with a meaningful glance at the cloth on his arm).

And when the door had closed—'We don't want anyone but the family,' he would mutter guiltily, becoming upright again. 'We don't want your mother excited.'

As on an island, behind a stone wall reinforced by high laburnums and lilac trees, they lived in a world of their

own, while outside the stream of cars and lorries flowed
ceaselessly.

In some miraculous way the big old cottage was always
bright and clean, with brass knobs shining, flowers from
the garden at the windows, curtains and covers always
fresh. Occasionally our mother would hoist herself up the
stairs with the help of the rail, beaming triumphantly as she
reached the top.

Then we would dust, going round all the rooms,
remarking on the pictures, the furniture, and the view from
the windows as if, up there, we were in some foreign
country.

✳   ✳   ✳

'That young fool of a doctor came to see your mother
today. He said I should live to be a hundred!' My father's
eyes were tragic. 'I told him straight out, "I just can't
afford to live to be a hundred." O dear! O dear!'

He turned and shuffled away, his shoulders bent, the
picture of dejection. But not before I had detected deep in
those deep-set eyes the ghost of a twinkle.

My mother, too, spoke of death.

'I shall never be able to die. I shouldn't know what to do
with Daddy. I shall just have to live for ever.'

✳   ✳   ✳

On Mondays I did the washing, hanging it out on the line
in the yard, and afterwards ironing it and putting it on the
clothes-horse by the fire. With sand-filled sausages at the
bottom of the doors and a good fire, the kitchen was quite
snug.

As I ironed, I edged the iron round the lace on my
mother's things and 'brought up' the embroidery in the
professional manner. I held out a night-dress for her to
admire my work.

'Yes, I've always liked that one, I'm using it sparingly. Is that a little hole? I'd better mend it right away.'

As I ironed, we talked, my father reading his book by the fire. Sometimes he would look up, tranquil and benign; satisfied because his wife was happy, being entertained, not in a draught and, for the moment, safe.

*   *   *

'Do you ever see that Mrs Waring?' my mother asked. 'You remember she had a 48-inch hip. She was having a very difficult time when I left the shop.'

'Yes, I saw her on the bus the other day. She looked better. There was a look on her face . . . smoothed out . . . she's too old to be in love . . . could she perhaps have been left some money do you think?'

'Yes, very likely. That would be it. I remember I saw in the paper that old Mrs Asquith had died. It was her aunt and she must have been rich: she used to have everything of the best—Chilprufe, I used to get it in specially . . . Yes, that would be it. How nice. It will make all the difference to her.

'. . . And I was wondering the other day about that Mrs Cuttle. Do you ever see her? She must be getting quite old now.'

'Yes, I saw her the other day. She's beginning to curl up. And her eyes . . . round the edge of the blue . . .'

'I know what you mean. As if they had been washed with a little soda in the water and the colour had run. Do you remember when that customer invited Daddy and me to tea and we forgot to go? It was during the war, and something happened, I can't remember what. Oh dear, I felt so awful . . . I shall never forget it. They had got everything ready, and were waiting. She had made blancmange.

'Do you remember that customer who thought she had

given me a pound note when she had only given me a ten shilling one? It was the only time in all those years that anything like that happened. Do you think . . . ? But no, I was quite, quite sure, because it was the only note I had in the till. But she was quite sure, too, and she never came in the shop again. She was such a nice person, and a very good customer.'

* * *

'That cat,' my mother said, 'is just like a human. When Daddy puts her into the shed at night she will take that little scarf Mary knitted for him, that he always wears when he gets the coal in; when he goes to let her out in the morning she's been sleeping on it. She gets on to the bottom of my bed, and then suddenly she gives a great leap and lands on my chest; I feel quite frightened, she's just like a tiger. She is always about. She sits and looks at me, and looks at me, and the only thing that seems strange is that she doesn't talk . . . sometimes I find myself thinking she will talk one day.' (The cat, which had appeared from nowhere, had unusual eyes, glowing, and curiously intent.)

'That cat is a poet. I saw her sitting out there for a long time the other evening—just watching the sun go down.'

The ground rose a little outside the casement window, and the cat would come to display mice she had caught. One day she brought a mole, still alive. She tossed it carelessly into the air, glancing indifferently in the opposite direction. Then her languid eye returned to the mole, which was digging with frantic haste. When it had almost disappeared from view, so well did it dig, the cat reached out a paw and again tossed it into the air.

The little drama produced to please us made our blood run cold. We banged on the window. But the cat ignored us—only laying a proprietary paw on the mole's back.

How could we stand by watching! (But the cat was so

proud.) Could we get round to the back of the house in time to take the mole away?

But it was all over. The mole was dead. There it lay, its little pink paws outstretched, and the cat walked off, the epitome of lofty unconcern.

✻   ✻   ✻

On Tuesdays the grocery man came for the order, sitting down to the kitchen table where there was always a cup of coffee and a piece of home-made cake, with a tray-cloth for the tray. Surreptitiously, with interest and pleasure, my father and mother watched him eat, as if he were a rare bird for whom they had spread out some very special crumbs.

Friday was a big day: the local paper and my mother's magazine came. It was also the day for going to the butcher, which meant a conference first about the joint. No doubt the most profitable piece was half a small leg of Canterbury lamb (knuckle end) but the butcher sometimes got nasty, saying people should remember that lambs have only two legs and he had the whole village to consider. Minced beef was a good buy; half a pound mixed with oatmeal, chopped onion, an Oxo cube, salt, pepper, and some water, and baked in the oven, went a long way. Then there were knuckles of bacon which could be simmered and the meat minced and mixed with parsley sauce.

At the weekend there might be visitors: little children whose lovely place of memory would always be there, the sun always shining; children who tore up and down the garden in an old Bath chair they had found in one of the sheds; gangling boys who jived together nonchalant and lively, to show how it was done; the little girl whose own father had died, sitting on her grandfather's knee to give his white hair 'a perm'; the nephew who came for the night, rising early the next morning to do a stint of digging before he went; the grandson who came in the holidays to help

143

with the painting. Then the aunts, now no longer able to detect the signs of poverty, who brought a copy of *Vogue*, or some flowers—carnations, perhaps, which would last for weeks in that cold, damp atmosphere.

'Do I look *much* older than she does?' my mother angled after the visit of the youngest aunt.

My father focused his eyes upon her.

'*You* look older than *her*? *You look older than her!* Why, next to her you look like a young bride.'

My mother gazed thoughtfully at her folded hands but could not hide her pleasure, or perhaps the tears in her eyes. After all, her husband was not given to lying, and certainly was not given to paying compliments.

*   *   *

They were living on dwindling capital, and I noticed that now, instead of the nylons my mother usually sent as presents, she gave her personal possessions: the ring holding the ruby which had come from the Ural Mountains; her grandmother's Paisley shawl; silk handkerchiefs which she had brought from the shop—till there was really nothing left.

They had always had an orange each with their breakfast; now they had one between them. My father, in a triumph of frugality, went further, cracking in two with one sharp blow from the back of the carving knife the Fox's glacier mint he had after lunch, so making one mint last for two days. His management of the fire, calculated to keep the room just warm enough but no more, was an art in itself. Then my mother told me that she had cancelled her magazine. 'I don't really need it,' she said. 'I have always got plenty of books to read.'

I tried to shake off a feeling, which persisted, of sunset, of completion, and of rounding off. All the cupboards upstairs were tidy; even my mother's desk, usually over-flowing, had been put in order.

＊　　　＊　　　＊

'That cat,' my mother said, 'is dead. She got run over, we think. She came in and lay on the kitchen floor—Daddy was in the garden. I couldn't lean down to her but I tried to stroke her with one of my sticks. She moved her tail a little bit, and then she died.'

Soon afterwards my mother had a severe stroke. My father hovered round as ambulance-men carried the stretcher through to the big sitting-room and set it down while they opened the front door, and as the morning sun streamed in the old man, oblivious of the doctor who was wanting to get to his next patient, and the ambulance-men who were in a hurry, knelt on the floor, and bending down, kissed the Rich Mrs Robinson gently on the forehead, embarked as she was on a journey he was soon to follow.